"The book focuses on an important promise of digital government, e-participation, which the authors rightly frame as the extension of public participation using ICTs. The book provides a much-needed emphasis on e-participation, with an international and comparative perspective on the factors enabling this phenomenon. The authors also offer important recommendations pertaining to regulations, skills, infrastructure, technological access and political mechanisms to foster an environment for enhanced e-participation."

Aroon Manoharan, *University of Massachusetts Boston*

"The Effects of Technology and Institutions on E-Participation: A Cross-National Analysis provides a new approach to examine and understand the factors that promote or constrain e-participation and its potential to increase democracy across the global community. This research expands the existing e-participation literature by combining theories of the policy process and information technology to examine the efficacy of e-participation. The findings from the study can provide policymakers and public managers a better understanding of the factors that facilitate citizen participation through the utilization of information and communication technology."

Luisa Diaz-Kope, *University of North Georgia*

"In a time when we are more connected than ever, for better, and worse; there is strikingly little consensus on how the public sector can best leverage technology toward a more democratic and participative society. Rawat and Morris ambitiously set out to address this cleavage by identifying factors that drive e-participation at a cross-national level. By emphasizing the role of institutions in driving e-participation, the authors provide a policy roadmap that will surely be of interest to policymakers and scholars interested in how to more effectively utilize technology to promote active and inclusive participation."

Martin Mayer, *The University of North Carolina at Pembroke*

T0347964

"This book offers an intriguing exploration of e-participation as a means for engaging public participation through the utilization of information and communication technology at a cross-country level. The unique framework developed by the authors incorporates policy feedback and socio-technical theories. Through the use of reputed international sources within a multivariate analysis, this model suggests factors related to political and regulatory environment combined with political rights and civil liberties can be brought together in different ways to foster e-participation across countries. This advancement of theory by Rawat and Morris will be of interest to scholars, students, and those interested in better understanding public participation mechanisms from an international perspective."

Madeleine Wright McNamara, *Tulane University*

"Pragati Rawat and John C. Morris have provided readers with an excellent analysis of cross-national e-participation – as a form of citizen engagement and as a public policy tool. The book is highly informative, relevant, well written, and eminently engaging. The findings and insights are particularly especially useful given ongoing policy challenges related diversity, equity, and inclusion, declining trust, sustainability, as well as the COVID-19 pandemic. In short, the book is an original contribution to the e-governance scholarship with important lessons for the future of citizen engagement."

Jonathan M. Fisk, *Auburn University*

The Effects of Technology and Institutions on E-Participation

In this book, Pragati Rawat and John C. Morris identify and evaluate the impact of factors that can help explain the difference in e-participation, public participation using information and communication technology, in different countries.

While cross-sectional studies have been covered, few have taken an in-depth look at cross-national studies. This book attempts to fill the gap using quantitative panel data to explore the influence of technology and institutions, and the impact of their complex relationships in a mediation and moderation analysis, on e-participation. The current study reviews the scholarly work in the field of "offline" and "online participation" to identify a set of antecedents that influence e-participation. A conceptual framework is developed, supported by the theories from the public policy and socio-technical premise. The authors utilize secondary data, primarily from the United Nations (UN) and World Economic Forum, for 143 countries from three waves of surveys to measure the dependent and explanatory variables. The panel data are statistically analyzed and findings reveal the role of technology as a mediator as well as a moderator for institutions' impact on e-participation.

The Effects of Technology and Institutions on E-Participation provides a groundbreaking country-level analysis that will appeal to academics and students of e-government and Digital Government, Public Policy, Public Administration, Public Sector Innovation, and Public Participation.

Pragati Rawat holds a PhD in Public Policy from Old Dominion University. An engineer and MBA from India, she has about 20 years of work experience in multinationals and government. Prior to joining the PhD program, she was engaged as a Process Manager in the Unique Identification program of the Government of India that created world's largest biometric database of residents for effective service delivery and inclusion. She has published articles in journals such as in *Politics & Policy, Journal of Environmental Studies and Sciences, Marine Technology Society Journal,* and *Public Works Management & Policy.*

John C. Morris is a Professor in the Department of Political Science at Auburn University. Prior to his appointment at Auburn, he held a joint appointment as a Professor of Political Science in the Department of Political Science and Geography, and a professor of public administration in the School of Public Service at Old Dominion University. He has published widely in public administration and public policy. He is the co-editor of *Speaking Green with a Southern Accent: Environmental Management and Innovation in the South* (2010), and *True Green: Executive Effectiveness in the US Environmental Protection Agency* (2012). He is also the co-editor of *Building the Local Economy: Cases in Economic Development,* published by the Carl Vinson Institute of Government, University of Georgia, in 2008; is the co-editor of a three-volume series (2012) on prison privatization, titled *Prison Privatization: The Many Facets of a Controversial Industry*; and *Advancing Collaboration Theory: Models, Typologies, and Evidence* (Routledge, 2016). His most recent books include *The Case for Grassroots Collaboration: Social Capital and Ecosystem Restoration at the Local Level* (2013, with William Gibson, William Leavitt, and Shana Jones); *State Politics and the Affordable Care Act: Choices and Decisions,* co-authored with Martin Mayer, Robert Kenter, and Luisa Lucero (Routledge, 2019); *Organizational Motivation for Collaboration: Theory and Evidence,* co-authored with Luisa Diaz-Kope (2019); *Better Together: Multiorganizational Arrangements for Watershed Protection,* co-authored with Madeleine W. McNamara (2021, Routledge); and *Policy Making and Southern Distinctiveness,* coauthored with Martin K. Mayer, Robert C. Kenter, and R. Bruce Anderson (2022; Routledge). His most recent book is *Clean Water Policy and State Choice: Promise and Performance in the Water Quality Act* (2022). In addition, he has published more than 70 articles in refereed journals, and nearly 40 book chapters, reports, and other publications.

Routledge Research in Public Administration and Public Policy

For more information about this series, please visit: www.routledge.com/Routledge-Research-in-Public-Administration-and-Public-Policy/book-series/RRPAPP

The Effects of Technology and Institutions on E-Participation

A Cross-National Analysis

Pragati Rawat and John C. Morris

Routledge
Taylor & Francis Group

NEW YORK AND LONDON

First published 2022
by Routledge
605 Third Avenue, New York, NY 10158

and by Routledge
2 Park Square, Milton Park, Abingdon, Oxon, OX14 4RN

Routledge is an imprint of the Taylor & Francis Group, an informa business

Library of Congress Cataloging-in-Publication Data
A catalog record for this title has been requested

ISBN: 978-0-367-75549-2 (hbk)
ISBN: 978-0-367-75861-5 (pbk)
ISBN: 978-1-003-16432-6 (ebk)

DOI: 10.4324/9781003164326

Typeset in Times New Roman
by Newgen Publishing UK

This book is dedicated to my late parents who instilled in me the value of education at a very early age. My loving husband, Abhishek, and my amazing daughter, Pakhi, have always been patiently by my side and supportive of all my ventures. –PR

This book is dedicated to my late parents, Charles H. and Mary B. Morris. –JCM

Contents

Figures

Tables

Acknowledgments

The authors extend their thanks to the anonymous reviewers who reviewed the prospectus and provided valuable feedback to improve this book. They thank the Senior Editor Natalja Mortensen and the Editorial Board at Routledge for believing in the idea of this book and giving them the green light to move forward. They also extend their many thanks to Editorial Assistant Charlie Baker for his support throughout the review and publication of this book, and special thanks to Luisa Diaz-Kope, University of North Georgia, for her assistance in evaluating the book chapters.

This book began as Pragati Rawat's dissertation at Old Dominion University. She thanks the dissertation committee members at Old Dominion University for their support through the original dissertation process. Dr. Yusuf was incredible and guided and supported Dr. Rawat throughout the PhD journey, and has made a lasting impression on her. She wishes to thank all the faculty and her peers at ODU, several of whom attended the proposal and dissertation defense and others who read the dissertation and contributed through their comments and questions. A special mention goes to Dr. Bill McCarthy who took out time to be at the dissertation defense and has had such a positive impression on her in their short interaction.

Acronyms

ANCOVA	Analysis of covariance
ANOVA	Analysis of variance
APA	Administrative Procedures Act
ASPA	American Society for Public Administration
C2G	Citizen-to-government
CLPM	Cross-lagged panel model
EIU	Economist Intelligence Unit
EPI	E-participation index
G2C	Government-to-citizen
HDI	Human Development Index
ICT	Information and communication technology
IPU	Inter-Parliamentary Union
IT	Information technology
ITU	International Telecommunication Union
NPM	New Public Management
NPR	National Performance Review
NPS	New Public Service
NRI	Network Readiness Index
OECD	Organization for Economic Co-operation and Development
OGD	Open Government Data
PFSTEP	A policy feedback and socio-technical approach to e-participation
SDG	Sustainable Development Goals
SEM	Simultaneous equation modeling
UCLA	University of California, Los Angeles
UID	Unique Identity
UN	United Nations

UNDESA	United Nations Department of Economic and Social Affairs
UNDPEPA	United Nations Division for Public Economics and Public Administration
UNPSA	United Nations Public Service Awards
WEF	World Economic Forum

1 The Importance of E-Participation as a Field of Study

The idea of public participation is not new (Dahl, 1989), and governments at all levels are increasingly adopting public participation in governing decisions (United Nations [UN], 2014). Public participation is a logical extension of the democratic process in more local, direct, deliberative ways (Brabham, 2009). Several mechanisms for public participation have been used across governments and recommended in the literature, for example, voting, sample surveys, public meetings, citizens' juries, and opinion polls (e.g., Delli Carpini et al., 2004; Rowe & Frewer, 2000; Smith, 2005; Verba, 1996). Participation "… also goes by a number of near synonyms such as engagement, involvement and empowerment, any of which may be prefaced by an adjective like public or community" (Smith & Dalakiouridou, 2009, p. 1). After the advent of information and communication technology (ICT), and especially after the growing popularity of the World Wide Web in the 1990s, there has been an emergent literature on the use and advantages of technology such as the internet and social networking sites in public participation (Fredericks & Marcus, 2013; Mossberger et al., 2008; Tolbert & Mossberger, 2006). This use of ICT in public participatory activities, known as e-participation, is the focus area of this study. The purpose of this book is to identify and evaluate the impact of institutional and technical factors that can help explain the difference in e-participation across countries. This book is designed to provide a new comprehensive framework for understanding the impact of the ICT resources and political institutions on online participation that can be applied to different countries.

E-participation is "the process of engaging citizens through ICTs in policy and decision-making in order to make public administration participatory, inclusive, collaborative and deliberative for intrinsic and instrumental ends" (UN, 2014, p. 61). The definition differs from e-government in that e-government is associated more with the use of

DOI: 10.4324/9781003164326-1

ICT for the provision of information and public services to the people (UN, 2014). The term "ICT" encompasses various computer and digital communication devices, applications, and services including internet, computers, radio, television, cell phones, computer networks, and satellite systems.

The UN has been assessing its member countries on an e-participation index since 2003; the study is now conducted biennially. The UN e-participation index measures the usage of a country's ICT infrastructure for the purpose of communicating government information to citizens such as policies and budgets, consulting with citizens for policymaking, and empowering people to provide their own inputs into government's decision making (UN, 2018). The assessment is done based on the availability of e-participation tools on national government portals for a set of criteria (UN, 2018). The UN recognizes that contextual factors, such as the telecommunication infrastructure, political will, human capital, and administration play important roles in the advancement of e-participation in a country (UN, 2014). However, one can observe countries with different levels of income, democracy, and technology status side by side in the UN e-participation survey results. This is intriguing, and it raises an important question: what explains the difference in the online participation between different countries? It is this curiosity that motivates the current study.

Why Study E-Participation?

Public participation is a core element of democracy (Lindner et al., 2016) and is considered a normative goal for inclusive communities that strengthens the legitimacy of governments and improves citizens' trust in public institutions (Le Blanc, 2020). E-participation is considered an important parameter of assessing open and accountable governments that helps build citizen trust in government (Peixoto & Fox, 2016; UN, 2019). Trust, in turn, has a positive influence on the use of ICT for public participation (Aichholzer & Rose, 2020). Citizens need to be treated not just as customers but as partners in the process to build effective governance (Kim & Lee, 2012). Studies argue that attempts to change attitude and behavior of individuals are more effective in a participatory environment; for example, efforts to change individual behaviors for a climate-friendly lifestyle are found to be more effective when they involve community participation (Aichholzer et al., 2016).

E-participation is considered a tool to strengthen the collaboration between government and citizens through use of ICT (UN, 2014). Web-based public participation ensures participation by a wider public and long-term sustainability by attracting and engaging youth (Rexhepi et al., 2018). The traditional offline public participation literature is fraught with the concerns of socioeconomic divide between those who do and do not participate. The same concern is found in the online public participation realm as well. The digital divide is the gap between those who have and those who do not have ICT and ICT skills. The ease of use of mobile devices and social media has been substantial in improving the accessibility to information and, thus, tackling the digital divide (Porwol & Ojo, 2017; UN, 2018).

E-participation, in its various forms, can contribute throughout the policymaking process, such as through e-petitions or online petitions in the problem definition stage and with e-consultations during the formulation stage (Lindner et al., 2016). Not only do the online platforms make it convenient for citizens to participate in political decision making by reducing their time and effort to participate but also reduce the information cost of participation by providing relevant information to a wide audience in a timely manner using tools such as web pages (Lindner et al., 2016). E-participation is also an essential tool for development and innovation in digital initiatives such as smart cities as ICT provides opportunities to the residents to participate in developing and testing smart government initiatives for addressing a range of social, economic, and environmental problems (Dameri, 2013; Guenduez et al., 2018).

Various international communities and forums have time and again encouraged governments to incorporate measures to enhance public participation and the value of public participation in attaining sustainable development (e.g., UN, 2000; World Public Sector Report, 2015; World Social Situation, 2016; World Summit on the Information Society, 2005). The sustainable development goals (SDG) 2030 specifically focus on participatory decision making particularly with reference to vulnerable individuals' groups and countries (SDG, 2020). For sustainable development, it is important that people are able to voice their concerns and participate in decisions that influence their lives and also that all countries are able to effectively participate in global decisions (SDG, 2020). SDG maintains that everyone is a user and provider of information and therefore countries are called upon to restructure their decision-making processes to assure broad participation. At the same time, governments at all levels are investing money in the ICT infrastructure. As per one report, the global ICT investment in government market is estimated at USD 431.15 billion in 2015 (Grand View Research, 2017). In the past decade, there has been a rapid improvement in e-participation tools and mechanisms offered by the governments across the world. It is also evident in the increased submissions by governments for the United Nations Public Service Awards (UNPSA) in 2018 and 2019 related to e-participation (Le Blanc, 2020). Half of these initiatives ensued at the national level, and most of all the initiatives pertain to advanced levels of e-participation in consulting, feedback, and agenda setting (Le Blanc, 2020).

Despite government investments in the ICT at all levels, researchers have maintained that the utilization of ICT infrastructure has not met its full potential, especially for e-participation (Le Blanc, 2020; Moon, 2002; Norris & Reddick, 2013; West, 2005). There are scholars skeptical of ICT's ability to change the landscape of public participation. Concerns about the digital divide hindering e-participation initiatives have existed since the early days of e-government (Le Blanc, 2020). As a result of the costs associated with public participation and the technical skills of the administrators themselves, public departments are left struggling to balance the varied and often conflicting goals of cost effectiveness with transparency involving information collection and dissemination (Viborg Andersen et al., 2007). The choice of an e-participation tool and its use is often impacted by political and institutional factors (Viborg Andersen et al., 2007). Despite the proliferation of online participation platforms, overall efforts to use citizen-led deliberations are limited (Porwol & Ojo, 2017). Although, e-participation has the potential for utilization throughout the policy process, it is mostly confined to the initial and final stages of the policy cycle and rarely do the citizen engagement feedback ingress into core decision-making stages (Van Dijk, 2012).

Participation is considered a defining characteristic of democracy; however, even authoritarian regimes have engaged in high levels of participation in some form, and participation may not necessarily lead to any particular type of democracy (Smith & Dalakiouridou, 2009). Some scholars, however, use e-participation and e-democracy interchangeably (e.g., Macintosh, 2008; Norris, 2007). Macintosh (2008) uses a single definition of e-participation and e-democracy "e-democracy and e- participation can be considered as the use of information and communication technologies to broaden and deepen political participation by enabling citizens to connect with one another and with their elected representatives" (p. 85). E-democracy mechanisms, such as online forums for deliberation, online voting, and online public consultation, are also the same as the mechanisms of e-participation. The current study does not engage in any comparison of the two terms and uses participation as it relates to public inputs to policy and decision making for political and policymaking purposes (see Smith & Dalakiouridou, 2009), which is consistent with UN's definition of e-participation.

Research Questions

Despite the faith in the digital medium to empower participation, various scholars over the years have pointed toward the lack of utilization of e-governance and internet in realizing their full democratic potential (Chadwick & May, 2003; Moon, 2002; Musso et al., 2000; West, 2005). Studies have evaluated the usage of, and motivators and barriers to, e-participation (Dawes, 2008; Jho & Song, 2015; Kukovič & Brezovšek, 2015; Norris & Reddick, 2013; Royo et al., 2014; Soonhee & Jooho, 2012; West, 2005). However, quantitative studies that have conducted a comparative analysis of multiple countries in e-participation are minimal (Jho & Song, 2015; Khan & Krishnan, 2020). The current study attempts to address this gap. The first research question that this paper seeks to answer is:

RQ1: What factors explain the difference in the degree of e-participation across countries?

Several studies have discussed offline and online public participation as a continuum with later stages attaining increasing complexity (e.g., Arnstein, 1969; Rowe & Frewer, 2000; UN, 2014). The UN e-government survey uses a three-level model of e-participation that moves from more passive to active engagement with people:

> 1) e-information that enables participation by providing citizens with public information and access to information upon demand, 2) e-consultation by engaging people in deeper contributions to and deliberation on public policies and services and 3) e-decision making by empowering people through co-design of policy options and co-production of service components and delivery modalities.
>
> (p. 63)

In addition to the overall e-participation index score, every member country is assigned a percentage utilization score for each of the three levels of e-participation (UN, 2014). Scholars (e.g., Van Dijk, 2012) have pointed out that the usage of ICT in e-participation is mainly limited in providing access to and exchange of politically relevant information (e-information) between the citizens and the government, and that there is hardly any perceived impact of public consultations (e-consultation) on policies and decision making (e-decision making). However, few e-participation studies have looked at difference of influence of factors across these stages. Do factors differ in their influence as one progresses from less complex to more complex stages of e-participation? The current study attempts to answer this question by using the stages of e-participation as defined in the UN e-Government Survey. Since e-participation stages are widely recognized in the literature, and the UN survey as well, this study additionally aims to assess the difference in the impact of factors for each level of e-participation. The second research question, therefore, is:

RQ2: Do the factors differ in their influence on e-information, e-consultation, and e-decision-making levels?

Why This Study?

Though there are several studies on adoption and diffusion of e-government and ICT in general, there are relatively few studies that examine the factors of e-participation. Still fewer are the studies that deal with a cross-country analysis of the e-participation dimension. The majority of studies in e-participation is single-country case studies, followed by some qualitative case comparisons and comparative studies within specific regions, and far fewer that explore e-participation on a global basis (Åström et al., 2012). Little research exists to answer how the use of ICT and/or institutions could influence distinctive outcomes on e-participation across countries (Jho & Song, 2015). Quantitative studies on e-participation, involving cross-country comparison on a global scale, are limited (Khan & Krishnan, 2020). Krishnan et al. (2017) categorize the e-participation literature into descriptive anecdotal studies, studies presenting demand side (citizen's perspective), and case studies involving micro-level analysis. As Krishnan et al. (2017, p. 298) state, "There is a dearth of macro-level quantitative empirical studies examining e-participation from the supply-side (i.e., government) perspective." Further, this study found that many of the quantitative cross-country studies use cross-sectional data, which is not considered to be optimal for deriving causation (Setia, 2016). Another criticism of scholarly work in the field of e-government is that it has been devoid of theory use and development (Heeks & Bailur, 2007). Furthermore, most e-participation studies lack a connect to the policy literature and have evaluated limited factors in frameworks studying direct and one-way impacts.

This book addresses these gaps by using macro-level supply-side data and stands apart from most of the previous studies as it not only proposes a conceptual model but quantitatively analyzes country level, i.e., macro-level, supply-side panel data to assess the impact of various technical and institutional factors on e-participation across countries. The study aims to evaluate the factors influencing e-participation in a cross-country analysis and do so by using a combination of public policy and technology theories. The study aims to generate insights about the factors that influence the degree and level of e-participation in a country.

Such a comparative analysis has several advantages. It improves the awareness and understanding about a country's institutions and resources in comparison to other countries, enables critical contrast with other countries, and provides wide range of alternatives for a country's problems by comparison with similar issues in other countries (Esser & Vliegenthart, 2017). The analysis also allows empirical testing across diverse countries that can contribute to development of theories that are universally applicable, but at the same time, the comparative analysis prevents scholars from overgeneralizing based on their own experiences and notions (Esser & Vliegenthart, 2017). By using panel data, the current study combines cross-territorial and cross-temporal dimensions (Esser & Vliegenthart, 2017) that has further advantages as it allows researchers to control for the effects of missing or unobserved variables (Hsiao, 2003). Due to greater sample variability and capturing inter-case as well as intra-case dynamics, panel data allow for more accurate inference of the model (Hsiao, 2003). Panel data allow one to account for the impact of phenomena or treatments that may not impact the dependent variable immediately (Hsiao, 2003), as happens in the case of most of the policy initiatives.

To measure the construct of e-participation, the current study uses the UN e-participation index data. This index is based on a qualitative assessment of online participatory services available in a country with respect to other member countries (UN, 2014). To identify the factors for e-participation, the scholarly work in the field of both "offline" and "online" participation (Gibson & Cantijoch, 2013, p. 701; Lim & Oh, 2016, p. 676; Smith, Schlozman et al., 2009, p. 1) is reviewed and discussed in the current study. Offline participation refers to participatory activities that are face to face or use mail, or letters, or phone as a medium; online participation or e-participation refers to the use of internet, social media, websites, or text and instant messaging as a medium for participatory activities (Smith, Schlozman et al. 2009). Drawing from this literature, a set of factors is identified, and a conceptual framework is developed for the study. The framework is supported by theories of public policy feedback and socio-technical premises. The framework is further assessed using secondary data from international sources of repute. The data are statistically analyzed and conclusions relevant for theory and practice are drawn from the results. The study helps discern the actions that different countries have taken and can take for promoting e-participation.

By using policy and technology theories, this book aims to gain better insights into the processes of e-participation and contribute to the knowledge of both theoretical frameworks. The practical contribution of the study is in policymaking. The findings guide governments and administrators on what factors are important and need to be promoted for encouraging e-participation. The findings also reveal the limitations of technology alone as a promoter of e-participation and suggest that both technology and institutional factors play an important role in facilitating use of ICT for participation.

Layout of This Book

The remaining chapters progress as follows: A detailed literature review is conducted next, followed by discussion of theories used in the current study, conceptual model development, and a data and analysis section with discussion of results. Rudestam and Newton (2007) talk about "long shots," "medium shots," and "close-ups" in a literature review (p. 68). For this study, the "long shot" is the public participation literature, the "medium shot" is the e-participation literature, and the "close-up" comprises of those studies that have conducted a quantitative cross-national analysis of e-participation similar to the current study.

Chapter 2 discusses the "long shot" area of literature in the current study – public participation (in offline mode). This discussion serves as the background for this project. In this case, it is important to understand the history and rise of public participation and the theoretical underpinnings of the literature. It helps place e-participation in the overarching literature of public participation and democracy. Therefore, the history and development of public participation are first discussed, along with some prevalent definitions of public participation, to give readers a basic framework for the concept of public participation. The subsections discuss why public participation is required, its levels, the critiques and concerns raised, factors impacting public participation as identified in the offline participation literature, and the approaches for public participation. It is important to identify the factors of offline participation in order to compare online participation factors to offline participation and to identify gaps in online participation literature. Technology is only a tool, and other contextual factors relevant for public participation can be important determinants of e-participation in a country.

Chapter 3 discusses the "medium shot" and "close-ups" in the literature review. The literature of e-participation is explored for the scope and general areas of research in e-participation. This section discusses what is meant by e-participation and details the three levels of e-participation and their assessment criteria as used by the UN survey. The types of studies in this section include e-participation, e-government, and public sector ICT adoption studies using quantitative or qualitative data analysis, conducted at any level of jurisdictions such as state or local governments, or involving one or few countries. Special focus is given to factors identified as determinants of e-participation, and factors for e-government or ICT adoption and diffusion. The analysis helps compare the offline literature with online literature, to detect the factors that are relevant in both, those that do not matter for online participation, and the ones that are relevant in an ICT-based scenario only.

The "close-up" literature discusses the studies that closely match the current study. It includes those studies that utilize quantitative data and statistical analysis for comparing multiple countries. These studies have utilized UN e-participation survey scores to measure their dependent variable. The explanatory and dependent variables, measures, and their data sources, and methodology used in these studies are presented. The gaps in the cross-country literature are identified based on the literature review.

Chapter 4 is a discussion of theories that leads to the development of a conceptual model for the current study. First, policy feedback theory is discussed, and the technology and institutional resources' relationship with e-participation is established. We follow this initial section with a discussion of socio-technical approaches to manifest the complex relationships of mediation and moderation between the technology and institutional resources. A conceptual model that establishes a policy feedback and socio-technical approach to e-participation (PFSTEP) is thus developed. Despite new technological developments and the rapid spread of e-participation, scholars are unsure if that has resulted in more participation (Le Blanc, 2020). Studies argue that, apart from ICT, the difference in politics and administration in each country influences participation (Jho & Song, 2015). The PFSTEP model hypothesizes that supporting institutional policies and administration and select ICT resources positively influence e-participation in a country. Additionally, the technology (ICT) resources act as a mediator as well as a moderator for the institutional resources' impact on e-participation. More than one dimension of technology and institutions are used in the model. The sources of data for measuring the dependent and explanatory variables are international surveys of UN and World Economic Forum that are used widely by scholars.

Chapter 5 discusses the impact of technology and institutional factors on e-participation. Data analysis and discussion of results, based on the measures used in the current study, are presented. It starts with a descriptive summary of data followed by results and discussion of mediation analysis, moderator analysis, and analysis for e-participation at different levels. The results highlight the role of specific dimensions of technology in mediating and moderating e-participation. The role of institutions is supported as an antecedent to technology. A summary of the test results for all hypotheses is presented.

Chapter 6 offers conclusion implications of the study for both practice and theory. One of the principles on which the UN's SDGs is based is public participation. ICT development, especially in terms of the internet, has provided a platform that governments worldwide have adopted for sharing information with the public for e-participation. Yet the success of e-participation varies widely across countries, and scholars have pointed to multiple factors. The current study results highlight the important role of institutions and select technology resources, such as ICT skills, in e-participation. ICT skills are increasingly understood as an important measure of the digital divide as merely accessing the resources of ICT is not sufficient, but the know-how to use the technology and, in the context of e-participation, to use the technology for the purpose of participation in government decision making is equally important. The role of policies and administrative quality in providing resources for political participation, as suggested by the results of the current study, informs the mechanisms of developing e-participation in a country. The areas ripe for governments to focus on are highlighted in this chapter. The findings of the study along with recent developments and long-term outlook on e-participation are shared.

References

Aichholzer, G., Feierabend, D., & Allhutter, D. (2016). Attitude and behavior changes through e-participation in citizen panels on climate targets. In G. Aichholzer, K. Herbert, & T. Lourdes (Eds.), *Evaluating e-participation: Frameworks, practice, evidence* (pp. 195–218). Cham: Springer, ProQuest Ebook Central.

Aichholzer, G., & Rose G. (2020) Experience with digital tools in different types of e-participation. In L. Hennen, I. van Keulen, I. Korthagen, G. Aichholzer, R. Lindner, & R. Nielsen (Eds.), *European e-democracy in practice: Studies in digital politics and governance* (pp. 93–140). Cham: Springer. https://doi.org/10.1007/978-3-030-27184-8_4.

Arnstein, S. (1969). A ladder of citizen participation. *Journal of the American Institution of Planners, 35*(4), 216–224.

Åström, J., Karlsson, M., Linde, J., & Pirannejad, A. (2012). Understanding the rise of e-participation in non-democracies: Domestic and international factors. *Government Information Quarterly, 29*(2), 142–150.

Brabham, D. C. (2009). Crowdsourcing the public participation process for planning projects. *Planning Theory, 8*(3), 242. Retrieved from http://plt.sage pub.com/cgi/content/abstract/8/3/242. Accessed on February 6, 2016.

Chadwick, A., & May, C. (2003). Interaction between states and citizens in the age of the internet: "E-government" in the United States, Britain, and the European Union. *Governance: An International Journal of Policy, Administration and Institutions, 16*(2), 271–300.

Dahl, R. A. (1989). *Democracy and its critics.* New Haven: Yale University Press.

Dameri, R. P. (2013). Searching for smart city definition: A comprehensive proposal. *International Journal of Computers & Technology, 11*(5), 2544–2551.

Dawes, S. S. (2008). The evolution and continuing challenges of e-governance. *Public Administration Review, 6*(8), S86–S102.

Delli Carpini, M. X., Cook, F. L., & Jacobs, L. R. (2004). Public deliberation, discursive participation, and citizen engagement: A review of the empirical literature. *Annual Review of Political Science, 7*(1), 315–344.

Esser, F., & Vliegenthart, R. (2017). Comparative research methods. In J. Matthes, C. S. Davis, & R. F. Potter (Eds.), *The international encyclopedia of communication research methods* (pp. 1–22). Hoboken, NJ: John Wiley & Sons, Inc. doi:10.1002/9781118901731.iecrm0035.

Fredericks, J., & Marcus, F. (2013). Augmenting public participation: Enhancing planning outcomes through the use of social media and web 2.0. *Australian Planner, 50*(3), 244–256.

Gibson, R., & Cantijoch, M. (2013). Conceptualizing and measuring participation in the age of the internet: Is online political engagement really different to offline? *Journal of Politics, 75*(3), 701–716.

Grand View Research. (2017). ICT Investment in government market size, share & trends analysis report by solution, by technology, by region, and segment forecasts, 2018–2025. Retrieved from www.grandviewresearch. com/industry-analysis/ict-investment-in-government-market. Accessed on October 15, 2020.

Guenduez, A. A., Singler, S., Tomczak, T., Schedler, K., & Oberli, M. (2018). Smart government success factors. *Swiss Yearbook of Administrative Sciences, 9*(1), 96–110.

Heeks, R., & Bailur, S. (2007). Analyzing e-government research: Perspectives, philosophies, theories, methods, and practice. *Government Information Quarterly, 24*(2), 43–265.

Hsiao, C. (2003). *Analysis of panel data* (2nd ed.). Cambridge: Cambridge University Press. https://doi.org/10.1017/CBO9780511754203.

Jho, W., & Song, K. J. (2015). Institutional and technological determinants of civil e-participation: Solo or duet? *Government Information Quarterly, 3*(2), 488–495.

Khan, A., & Krishnan, S. (2020). Virtual social networks diffusion, governance mechanisms, and e-participation implementation: A cross-country investigation. *E-Service Journal, 11*(3), 36–69. doi:10.2979/eservicej.11.3.02.

Kim, S., & Lee, J. (2012). E-participation, transparency, and trust in local government. *Public Administration Review, 72*(6), 819–828.

Krishnan, S., Teo, T., & Lymm, J. (2017). Determinants of electronic participation and electronic government maturity: Insights from cross-country data. *International Journal of Information Management, 37*(4), 297–312.

Kukovič, S., & Brezovšek, M. (2015). E-democracy and e-participation in Slovenian local self-government. *Croatian & Comparative Public Administration, 15*(2), 451–474.

Le Blanc, D. (2020). E-participation: A quick overview of recent qualitative trends. UN DESA Working Paper No. 163 ST/ESA/2020/DWP/163. Retrieved from www.un.org/esa/desa/papers/2020/wp163_2020.pdf. Accessed on June 1, 2020.

Lim, S., & Oh, Y. (2016). Online versus offline participation: Has the democratic potential of the internet been realized? Analysis of a participatory budgeting system in Korea. *Public Performance & Management Review, 39*(3), 676–700.

Lindner, R., Aichholzer, G., & Hennen, L. (2016). *Electronic democracy in Europe: Prospects and challenges of e-publics, e-participation and e-voting.* Cham: Springer, ProQuest Ebook Central.

Macintosh, A. (2008). E-democracy and e-participation research in Europe. In H. Chen et al. (Eds.), *Digital government, integrated series in information systems* (Vol. 17, pp. 85–102). Boston, MA: Springer. https://doi.org/10.1007/978-0-387-71611-4_5.

Moon, M. (2002). The evolution of e-government among municipalities: Rhetoric or reality? *Public Administration Review, 62*(4), 424–433.

Mossberger, K., Tolbert, C. J., & McNeal, R. S. (2008). *Digital citizenship: The internet, society, and participation*: Cambridge, MA: MIT Press.

Musso, J., Weare, C., & Hale, M. (2000). Designing web technologies for local governance reform: Good management or good democracy? *Political Communication, 17*(1), 1–19.

Norris, D. F. (2007). E-democracy and e-participation among local governments in the United States, E-participation and e-government: Understanding the present and creating the future. Report of the ad hoc expert group meeting, Budapest, Hungary, July 27–28, 2006, pp. 147–170.

Norris, D. F., & Reddick, C. G. (2013). Local e-government in the United States: Transformation or incremental change? *Public Administration Review, 73*(1), 165–175.

Peixoto, T., & Fox, J. A. (2016). When does ICT-enabled citizen voice lead to government responsiveness? Digital dividends: Background paper for the World Development Report 2016. https://doi. org/10.19088/1968-2016.104.

Porwol, L., & Ojo, A. (2017). Barriers and desired affordances of social media based e-participation – politicians' perspectives. ICEGOV '17: Proceedings of the 10th International Conference on Theory and Practice of Electronic Governance – March 2017 (pp. 78–86). https://doi.org/10.1145/3047273.3047324.

Rexhepi, A., Filiposka, S., & Trajkovik, V. (2018). Youth e-participation as a pillar of sustainable societies. *Journal of Cleaner Production, 174*, 114–122.

Rowe, G., & Frewer, L. J. (2000). Public participation methods: A framework for evaluation. *Science, Technology, and Human Values, 25*(1), 3–29.

Royo, S., Yetano, A., & Acerete, B. (2014). E-participation and environmental protection: Are local governments really committed? *Public Administration Review, 74*(1), 87–98.

Rudestam, K., & Newton, R. (2007). *Surviving your dissertation a comprehensive guide to content and process* (3rd ed.). Los Angeles, CA: Sage.

Setia, M. S. (2016). Methodology series module 3: Cross-sectional studies. *Indian Journal of Dermatology, 61*(3), 261–264.Smith, A., Schlozman, K. L., Verba, S., & Brady, H. (2009). The demographics of online and offline political participation. Retrieved from www.pewinternet.org/2009/09/01/the-demographics-of-online-and-offline-political-participation/. Accessed on April 24, 2018.

Smith, G. (2005). *Beyond the ballot, 57 democratic innovations from around the world.* London: The Power Inquiry.

Smith, S., & Dalakiouridou, E. (2009). Contextualising public (e)participation in the governance of the European Union. *European Journal of ePractice, 7*, 1–9.

Soonhee, K., & Jooho, L. (2012). E-participation, transparency, and trust in local government. *Public Administration Review, 72*(6), 819–828.

Sustainable Development Goals (SDG). (2020). Information for integrated decision-making & participation. Retrieved from https://sustainabledeve lopment.un.org/topics/information-integrated-decision-making-and-partic ipation. Accessed on October 10, 2020.

Tolbert, C. J., & Mossberger, K. (2006). The effects of e-government on trust and confidence in government. *Public Administration Review, 66*(3), 354–369.

United Nations (UN). (2000). Millennium declaration. Retrieved from www. un.org/en/development/devagenda/millennium.shtml. Accessed on May 5, 2021.

United Nations (UN). (2014). E-government survey 2014. Retrieved from http://unpan3.un.org/egovkb/Portals/egovkb/Documents/un/2014-Survey/ E-Gov_Complete_Survey-2014.pdf. Accessed on October 11, 2015.

United Nations (UN). (2018). E-government survey 2018. Retrieved from www. un.org/development/desa/publications/2018-un-e-government-survey.html. Accessed on June 3, 2020.

United Nations (UN). (2019). World public sector report. Retrieved from https://publicadministration.un.org/publications/content/PDFs/World%20 Public%20Sector%20Report2019.pdf. Accessed on June 3, 2020.

Van Dijk, J. A. G. M. (2012). Digital democracy: Vision and reality. In I. Snellen, W. Thaens, & W. van de Donk (Eds.), *Public administration in the information age: Revisited* (pp. 49–61). Amsterdam: IOS-Press.

Verba, S. (1996). The citizen as respondent: Sample surveys and American democracy. *American Political Science Review, 90*, 1–7.

Viborg Andersen, K., Zinner Henriksen, H., Secher, C., & Medaglia, R. (2007). Costs of e-participation: The management challenges. *Transforming Government: People, Process and Policy, 1*(1), 29–43.

West, D. (2005). *Digital government technology and public sector performance* (Safari tech books online). Princeton, NJ: Princeton University Press.

World Public Sector Report. (2015). Retrieved from https://publicadministrat ion.un.org/en/Research/World-Public-Sector-Reports. Accessed on May 5, 2021.

World Social Situation. (2016). Retrieved from www.un.org/development/ desa/dspd/2015/12/30/report-on-world-social-situation-2016/#more-10405. Accessed on May 5, 2021.

World Summit on the Information Society. (2005). Tunis agenda for the infor- mation society. Retrieved from www.itu.int/net/wsis/docs2/tunis/off/6rev1. html. Accessed on May 5, 2021.

2 Public Participation

What Is Public Participation?

The idea of public participation in governing decisions has been prevalent from ancient times. Evidence from Rig-Veda (1700 BCE) suggests that self-governing village bodies called "sabhas" and "samitis" existed in the remote past (Das, 2014). In Athenian Greece, the idea and practice of rule by the many, as opposed to rule by the few, is known to have persisted (Dahl, 1989). In the 1830s and 1840s in Britain, a movement appeared calling for a revivification of decentralized government followed by the rise of populist politics (Inscape, 2013). By the 1960s, driven by mass youth movements, enormous gatherings in public, mass media, and political ideas around civil society, a new theory of democratic participation evolved as a renewed vision of democracy (Inscape, 2013). In the United States, reforms under the New Deal (1933–1938) included the Administrative Procedures Act (APA) that became a law in 1946. The APA required agencies to keep the public informed of their organization, procedures, and rules and provide for public participation in the rulemaking process (National Archives, 2016). Later reforms such as the Freedom of Information Act (1966) and the Privacy Act (1974) were steps toward strengthening public engagement in public policies.

Scholars have cited several theoretical arguments that support the rise of political participation. The new public service (NPS) literature credits interpretive theory (Harmon, 1981), critical theory (Denhardt, 1981), and postmodern (McSwite 1997; Miller & Fox, 2007) approaches to collectively shape public organizations less dominated by issues of authority and control and more by the needs and concerns of employees, clients, and citizens (Denhardt & Denhardt, 2000). Moynihan (2003) cites postmodern discourse theory, disillusionment with bureaucracy, and the search for a democratic ideal that contributes to the rise of political participation. Public discourse as a means to

DOI: 10.4324/9781003164326-2

find solutions in participatory policies in place of the bureaucratic structures identifies with the postmodern discourse theory (Moynihan, 2003). Cross-time and cross-national surveys are evidence of a shift to postmodern age that includes a desire for more participatory democracies (Inglehart, 1980).

The roots of public participation can be found in the democracy literature. The traditional governmental system was criticized as producer dominated and bureaucratic, which gave support to the idea that networks and partnerships have participatory and democratic potential and market or quasi-market innovations are a means of expanding participatory democracy (McLaverty, 2011). The approach resulted in measures associated with new public management (NPM), but here the public was empowered as a consumer and not as a democratic citizen (Denhard & Denhardt, 2000; McLaverty, 2011). Other scholars saw decentralization of control over neighborhoods and services as "bottom up" democracy to engage with citizens, particularly with historically marginalized groups (McLaverty, 2011). Due to declining participation in traditional types of politics (Dalton, 2004), and the evidence of declining trust in political regimes, the interest in ideas of governance began to grow and governments began to look for new mechanisms of political participation (McLaverty, 2011). As a consequence of public sector reform, the technological revolution, devolution, as well as globalization, the traditional state methods of command and control gave way to more flexible and inclusive modes of state–citizen interaction (Le Gales, 2011). Increased education leads to greater demand for involvement and access to information (Thomas, 1995), and access to information is facilitated by new technologies (Moynihan, 2003).

Several definitions, continua, sets of characteristics, and descriptions exist for indicating the type and level of public involvement in communities and government. The examples range from Habermas' (1992) idea of public sphere of like-minded citizens debating equally in an open public arena, to Arnstein's (1969) ladder with eight rungs of citizen participation that juxtaposes powerless citizens with the powerful; to Beetham's (1993) democracy continuum; and Smith's (2005) *57 Democratic Innovations from Around the World* (also the report's subtitle). King et al. (1998) consider "authentic participation" (p. 317) as the effective form of participation that moves the administrator away from a reliance on technical and expertise models of administration and toward meaningful participatory processes. Some of the terms and their definitions, in practice, that indicate citizen involvement in public decision-making activities are as follows:

Citizen participation is the redistribution of power that enables the have-not citizens, presently excluded from the political and economic processes, to be deliberately included in the future, in determining how information is shared, goals and policies are set, tax-resources are allocated, programs are operated, and benefits like contracts and patronages are parceled out.

(Arnstein, 1969)

Political participation is the "legal acts by private citizens that are more or less directly aimed at influencing the selection of governmental personnel and/or the actions they take."

(Verba et al., 1978, p. 1)

Public participation encompasses a group of procedures designed to consult, involve, and inform the public to allow those affected by a decision to have an input into that decision.

(Smith, 1983, as cited in Rowe & Frewer, 2000, p. 6)

Citizen participation involves "to inform, consult, engage, and collaborate with citizens" (Lukensmeyer & Torres, 2006, p. 7) while citizen engagement "is a commitment from government to cultivate deeper levels of knowledge among citizens generally about the issue at hand and potential solutions and to provide opportunities for citizens to exercise that knowledge in service of policy and program development in a regular and ongoing basis."

(Lukensmeyer & Torres, 2006, p. 8)

(Citizen participation) implies the involvement of citizens in a wide range of policymaking activities, including the determination of levels of service, budget priorities, and the acceptability of physical construction projects in order to orient government programs toward community needs, build public support, and encourage a sense of cohesiveness within neighborhoods.

(United Nations [UN], 2008, p. 4)

The definitions vary to a large extent, and several terms are used by scholars, such as citizen engagement, public participation, and political participation (Lim & Oh, 2016). Ekman and Amna (2012) discuss how the initial definitions of citizen engagement were focused on participation in elections, while later and more recent definitions point out actions of ordinary citizens to influence government decisions "in-between elections" (p. 286) such as defined by Verba et al. (1978). Developing their own comprehensive typology of political participation, they (Ekman & Amna, 2012) list latent (e.g., personal interest and attentiveness toward political issues, sense of belonging to a group) and manifest forms (e.g., casting ballots, signing petitions, membership of political parties) of political participation at individual and collective levels as well as illegal forms of participation such as violent activities and protests. Public participation has often been equated with a more continuous involvement in shaping policies and public service delivery than one-time voting (UN, 2014). For the purpose of the current study, public participation and citizen engagement is used interchangeably and is used to refer to procedures to inform, consult, and involve citizens in order for them to be able to participate in public policymaking and decision making (as in Smith, 1983; UN, 2008, 2014).

Why Is Public Participation Important?

Public participation can be seen as a logical extension of the democratic process in more local, direct, and deliberative ways (Brabham, 2009). At the very least, involving citizens in the planning process helps ensure a plan that will be more widely accepted by its future users (Burby, 2003, as cited in Brabham, 2009). Some see the rise in public participation as a shift from government to governance where *government* refers to actions backed by legally and formally derived authority and policing power, and *governance* refers to sharing power in decision making and actions backed by the shared goals of citizens and organizations, who may or may not have formal authority and policing power (Van der Arend & Behagel, 2011).

Public policy decisions impact several people. Copious reasons have been quoted for citizen participation in public decision making. The reasons for public participation can be divided into two categories. The first category points to the issues in the traditional governmental system such as limited knowledge of the experts, elites concealing or ignoring risks, issues of elite or special interests and domination by them, the public's rejection of expert's claims, and disillusionment with government (Horlick-Jones et al., 2007; Moynihan, 2003; Rowe & Frewer, 2000). The second category points toward the benefits of public participation. Burton et al. (2004) argue that involvement is a basic right; it overcomes alienation, makes the community stronger, maximizes the effectiveness of services and resources, helps conjoin different contributions to development, and helps sustainability. Better understanding of problems, multiplicity of ideas for solving them, public education and control, development of a sense of citizenship, public support for implementation, building public perceptions of fairness and trust in the authorities, and formation of responsive and accountable states are other benefits cited in participation studies (e.g., Horlick-Jones et al., 2007; International Peacebuilding Advisory Team [IPAT], 2015; Tolbert & Mossberger, 2006). Deliberation is also expected to lead to greater empathy with others and is considered a normative good (Delli Carpini et al., 2004). Webler (1999) contends that one of the most cited reasons for why there should be citizen participation is that it improves decisions. Rowe and Frewer (2000) claim that the most persuasive argument for public involvement is that the public is theoretically able to play a role in risk management at most, if not all, stages of policy.

Levels of Participation

Several scholars have attempted to define a continuum of different levels of public participation. One of the seminal works in this area is Sherry Arnstein's (1969) ladder of citizen participation with eight rungs, which juxtaposes powerless citizens with the powerful. The bottom most rungs indicate non-participation (contrived as participation) techniques and as one goes up the ladder, the participation improves from merely informing and consulting citizens to delegating power to citizens, and eventually citizen control when have-nots obtain the decision-making seats, partially or fully (Arnstein, 1969).

Beetham (1993) argues that at one end of the democracy continuum is complete direct democracy, where all decisions are made by all participants, and at the other end is complete autocracy with democratic systems falling somewhere in between the two extremes. Another argument is that the lowest level of public involvement employs top-down communication and a one-way flow of information, while the highest level is characterized by active participation in the decision-making process (Rowe & Frewer, 2000). Citizen participation (referred to as a more general term) and engagement have been differentiated by some scholars (e.g., Lukensmeyer & Torres, 2006). To simply inform and to consult are considered as participatory techniques, while citizen engagement is an active, intentional partnership between the general public and decision makers, that engages and empowers citizens, is fundamentally knowledge building, and can have profoundly positive benefits to policy development and the citizens' view of government (Lukensmeyer & Torres, 2006). Further, citizen engagement is considered as "... part of a family of democratic reform ideas that includes public participation, public involvement, participatory democracy, deliberative democracy, and collaborative governance" (Lukensmeyer & Torres, 2006, p. 9). Thus, despite the differences in how scholars define the levels of participation, there is a general agreement in these studies about public participation that it has levels or stages of development.

Concerns, Critiques, and Challenges of Public Participation

Despite the foregoing benefits of public participation, there are studies that question, debate, or instigate future research on the usefulness of public participation (Irvin & Stansbury, 2004; Kingston et al., 2000; Webler, 1999). Concerns are often raised about the legitimacy of citizen participation as the participants are not necessarily representative of the general population, have no authorization or accountability toward the public, and the way their inputs feed into policy decision making is unclear (McLaverty, 2011). In a seminal article, Arnstein (1969) emphasized the importance of redistribution of power, in order to empower the powerless as essential for public participation, in the absence of which the participatory exercises are sham or non-participation. Who participates, who controls the agenda, and whether the decision makers respond to the outcomes of public participation are underscored as major concerns and criticisms against public participation (Innes & Booher, 2004; McLaverty, 2011; Parry & Moyser 1994; Rowe & Frewer, 2000; Webler, 1999). Whether or not the participants are representative of the public as a whole is a matter of concern (Verba et al., 1993). Other criticisms raised are related to making unreasonable demands on people's time, reducing complex issues to a "yes or no" decision such as in referenda, lack of expertise of members of the general public, and time and cost investments (McLaverty, 2011). Challenges for public participation are studied from the institutional as well as the citizen perspective. Often the institutional, rather than the technological, issues hinder greater participation (Ganapati, 2011). Public participation is limited by political structures, opposition from local leaders and administrators, organizational culture, availability of human resources, and relationships between government and non-governmental agencies (Falco & Kleinhans, 2018; Ganapati, 2011; McLaverty, 2011; Parry & Moyser 1994).

Lowndes et al. (2001) reported the findings drawn from 30 focus group discussions carried out with citizens in 11 contrasting local authority areas in Britain, probing the views of citizens themselves about the prospect and reality of public participation. The reasons reported by citizens for non-participation were a negative view of the local authority as well as the councilors, citizens' perception (or experience) of a lack of council response to consultation, lack of even acknowledgment of receipt of complaint, the length of time taken to resolve an issue, and the perfunctory nature of the solutions provided (Lowndes et al., 2001). Many involved in the focus groups expressed that they felt excluded based on who they were and that certain people always dominated in the participation (Lowndes et al., 2001). Lack of trust in participatory processes and government agencies is cited as hindrances to public participation in other studies as well (e.g., Beierle & Konisky, 2000; Brown et al., 2002; Lee & Schachter, 2019). Some scholars raise the "dark side" (Putnam, 2000, p. 350) of public participation in political decision making (e.g., Bouchard, 2016; Meijer et al., 2009) or implementation, for example, participation by extremist groups or people intending to violate policies can result in undermining democratic regimes and a decrease in compliance with government rules (Meijer et al., 2009).

Some recommendations for overcoming the challenges of public participation include strategic planning of engagement activities (Mergel, 2013), one-stop shops that are open all day where people can register their issues or suggestions, long-term community development objectives, informing residents of outcomes, good customer care, direct invitations and appropriate incentives, and employment of different methods for involving different groups (Lowndes et al., 2001), availability of information in different languages, quality and reliable data, data management, and guaranteeing privacy and security (Bertot et al., 2012). Relevant, accessible, and timely information and a two-way feedback system where the governments not only ask for citizen inputs but are also accountable to provide information on what they did with the citizen inputs are central to citizen engagement (Rajani, n.d.). Political knowledge, interest, efficacy, trust, and democratic attitudes are posited to increase participation, and participation is also considered to facilitate a positive change in knowledge and attitudes (Moehler, 2007).

Factors Impacting Public Participation

In the context of (offline) public participation, seminal studies examine a range of socioeconomic and demographic factors and role of institutions in citizen's level of participation in politics and policy. Verba et al. (1995) identify three important resources of time, income, and civic skills as important predictors of public participation. Findings from their studies suggest that higher levels of socioeconomic resources such as education and income lead to higher levels of political participation

(Verba, 1996; Verba et al., 1978, 1995). In a cross-national study of seven countries, Verba et al. (1978) argue that institutions, such as political parties, trade unions, ethnic and religious organizations, and neighborhood associations play an interfering role between an individual's socioeconomic status and participation (measured as voting, campaign, and communal activity). The poor lack civic skills that impacts their participation levels and inequality thus impacts participation (Verba et al., 1995). Institutions such as churches help develop these skills (Verba et al., 1995). Moynihan (2003) also raises the concern of full and representative participation in civic summits. Administrative values and how managers organize participation are important determinants of full and representative participation, and the willingness to employ meaningful participation increases at the time of a crisis (Moynihan, 2003). Rosenstone and Hansen (1993) emphasize mobilization as the key resource for participation, while Verba et al.'s (1995) study argues for recruitment, where the former is the political approach focusing on the role of political institutions and elites, and the latter is the sociological approach that focuses on community organizations (Mettler & Soss, 2004).

Putnam (2000) looked at changes in family structure, women's roles, suburban life, work, age, television, computers, and other factors that contributed to the decline in the stock of social capital, which in turn generated an individual's disconnect with democratic structures (apart from family and friends). Verba and Nie (1972) argue that participants and non-participants differ in how they view problems and the solutions to those problems, and their study of public participation in America includes a wide range of explanatory variables such as size of city, race, gender, age, income, religion, location, ethnic groups, and their mobilizing agents (Verba & Nie, 1972). Webler (1999) concludes that citizens will not participate unless the issues are tangible, significant in their view, or they feel that their participation will make a difference. While some consider the tendency of groups to pursue private interests and that incentivizing individuals may promote participation (Olson, 1965), others rely on solidarity and public spiritedness, and place less importance to self-interest as a motivator (Lowndes et al., 2001; Putnam, 2000).

Citizens become involved in politics when they have resources enabling them to participate, attitudes motivating them to participate, and people asking them to participate (Verba et al., 1995). Nearly all models of participation take into account individual-level demographic characteristics and resources; most consider attitudes, and far fewer incorporate recruitment or mobilization as important factors of participation (Leighley, 1995). The impact of mobilization factors on participation has been studied to a lesser extent as compared to attitude and mechanisms. Moehler (2007) examines how participation is impacted by mobilization factors using measures such as the respondents' relationships to the government councils, civil society, and community, as well as the probability that the respondents received messages from program organizers. Verba and Nie (1972) study the impact of collectivities (ethnic groups) and their mobilizing agents, such as labor unions, on public participation. In another study, Verba et al. (1995) develop a civic voluntarism model that considers resources (time, money, and civic skills), psychological engagement with politics (political efficacy explained as an individual's belief that s/he can make a difference), and access to recruitment as important antecedents to political participation. Downs (1957), in his seminal article, highlighted the role and power of "persuaders" over those who are rationally ignorant (p. 139). The voters do not have full knowledge about the action of the government, and persuaders present them with a biased selection of facts that influences the voter's decision. Government, on the other hand, does not know what citizens want and needs representatives to persuade citizens to re-elect them. Apathy of citizens toward elections is a result of imperfect information (due to the high costs of information in the real world), and at the same time, government decision making is contextual and depends on a society's political constitution – the power relationship between the governors and those governed (Downs, 1957). Some seminal studies and the list of factors for offline participation discussed here are presented in Table 2.1.

Mechanisms of Public Participation

Several mechanisms for public participation have been used and recommended in the literature. In his report *Beyond the Ballot*, Graham Smith (2005) outlines *57 Democratic Innovations from Around the World* (also the report subtitle), grouped around six headings: electoral innovations (e.g., postal ballots, public opinion surveys, compulsory voting, and reducing the voting age); consultation innovations (e.g., standing forums, public meetings, and opinion surveys); deliberative innovations (e.g., citizens' juries, deliberative opinion polls, consensus conferences, and deliberative mapping); co-governance innovations (e.g., participatory budgeting, giving citizens places on partnership boards, and citizens' assemblies); direct democracy innovations (e.g., referendums); and e-democracy innovations. Rowe and Frewer (2000) mention referenda, public hearings, public opinion surveys, consensus conference, citizen's jury, focus groups, negotiated rulemaking, and

Table 2.1 List of factors for offline participation

Explanatory variables in (offline) participation studies	Study
Institutions; mandates; administrative systems and processes	Arnstein (1969); King et al. (1998); Moynihan (2003);
Instrumental factors such as administrative costs and perceived benefits; modes/tools for participation (such as surveys) and participation forums	King et al. (1998); Moynihan (2003); Verba (1996)
Administrator – reeducation of public managers; existing values of administrators; administrative self-interest costs such as loss of influence; how seriously managers take public input	Lowndes et al. (2001); Moynihan (2003)
Social capital – Changes in work, family structure, women's roles; suburban life; role of television, computers; or citizens' involvement in family, work, school, and religion	Putnam (2000); Verba and Nie (1972)
Mobilizing agents/recruiters – belonging to an organization; collectivities (ethnic groups) and their mobilizing agents (labor unions, parties); social and political institutions (political parties and organizational systems such as trade unions, ethnic and religious organizations, and neighborhood associations); access to recruitment networks; role of persuaders; respondents' relationships to the government councils, civil society, and community, and the probability that the respondents received messages from program organizers	Downs (1957); Moehler (2007); Verba (1996); Verba and Nie (1972); Verba et al. (1978, 1995)
Resources: time, money (or income), civic skills	Verba (1996); Verba and Nie (1972); Verba et al. (1995)
Citizen attitudes such as psychological engagement with politics like political efficacy (the belief that they can make a difference); views and perceptions about the local authority; level of trust in participatory processes; difference in participants' and non-participants' views of problems and solutions	Brown et al. (2002); Lowndes et al. (2001); Verba and Nie (1972); Verba et al. (1995); Webler (1999)
Socioeconomic, demographic: age, education, race, sex, religion, location, size of city	Putnam (2000); Verba (1996); Verba and Nie (1972)
Information: imperfect information, cost of information	Downs (1957)

Table 2.1 Cont.

Explanatory variables in (offline) participation studies	Study
Rationality: political party's private interests, incentives, type of issue	Downs (1957); Olson (1965); Webler (1999)
Solidarity, public spiritedness	Lowndes et al. (2001); Moynihan (2003); Putnam (2000)

citizen advisory committees as public participation techniques. The mechanisms used for participation include individual decisions to vote or abstain, individual campaign, and communal activity (e.g., Verba et al., 1978), contacting officials, giving money, sitting on a local board, joining a group, and protesting (e.g., Verba et al. (1995). Delli Carpini et al. (2004) argue that participation can involve private individuals in informal, unplanned exchanges; those who convene for public purposes but do so outside the normal processes of government operations (for example, in such places as libraries, schools, homes, churches, and community centers); and those who are brought together in settings such as town hall meetings of political representatives and their constituents. Discursive participation can occur through a variety of media, including face-to-face exchanges, phone conversations, email exchanges, and internet forums (Delli Carpini et al., 2004).

Since the surge in popularity of the World Wide Web in the 1990s, there has been a growing literature on electronic participation (*e-participation*). E-participation is participation using information and communication technologies (ICTs) and encompasses activities such as informing public of government activities, consultation with public for policy issues and decision making, and empowering them for decision making (UN, 2014) through online modes such as websites, social media, and mobiles. Chapter 3 discusses e-participation and factors that influence it.

References

Arnstein, S. (1969). A ladder of citizen participation. *Journal of the American Institution of Planners, 35*(4), 216–224.

Beetham, D. (1993). Liberal democracy and the limits of democratization. In D. Held (Ed.), *Prospects for democracy: North, south, east, west* (pp. 53–73). Oxford: Polity Press.

Beierle, T. C., & Konisky, D. M. (2000). Values, conflict, and trust in participatory environmental planning. *Journal of Policy Analysis and Management, 19*(4), 587–602.

Bertot, J. C., Jaeger, P. T., & Hansen, D. (2012). The impact of polices on government social media usage: Issues, challenges, and recommendations. *Government Information Quarterly, 29*(1), 30–40. http://dx.doi.org/10.1016/j.giq.2011.04.004.

Bouchard, N. (2016). The dark side of public participation: Participative processes that legitimize elected officials' values. *Canadian Public Administration Publique du Canada, 59*(4), 516–537. https://doi.org/10.1111/capa.12199.

Brabham, D. C. (2009). Crowdsourcing the public participation process for planning projects. *Planning Theory, 8(3)*, 242. Retrieved from http://plt.sagepub.com/cgi/content/abstract/8/3/242. Accessed on February 6, 2016.

Brown, K., Adger, W. N., & Tompkins, E. L. (2002). *Making waves: Integrating coastal conservation and development*. London: Routledge.

Burby, R. J. (2003). Making plans that matter: Citizen involvement and government action. *Journal of the American Planning Association, 69*(1), 33–49.

Burton, P., Goodlad, R., Croft, J., Abbott, J., Hastings, A., Macdonald, G., & Slater, T. (2004). What works in community involvement in area-based initiatives? A systematic review of the literature. Online Report 53/04. London: Home Office. Retrieved from http://webarchive.nationalarchives.gov.uk/20110218135832/http:/rds.homeoffice.gov.uk/rds/pdfs04/rdsolr5304.pdf. Accessed on January 24, 2016.

Dahl, R. A. (1989). *Democracy and its critics*. New Haven, CT: Yale University Press.

Dalton, R. (2004). *Democratic challenges, democratic choices: The erosion in political support in advanced industrial democracies*. Oxford: Oxford University Press.

Das, P. K. (2014). History of local self-government in ancient India and under the British rule. *Asian Journal of Multidisciplinary Studies, 2*(11), 79–83.

Delli Carpini, M. X., Cook, F. L., & Jacobs, L. R. (2004). Public deliberation, discursive participation, and citizen engagement: A review of the empirical literature. *Annual Review of Political Science, 7*(1), 315–344.

Denhardt, R. B. (1981). *In the shadow of organization*. Lawrence, KS: Regents Press of Kansas.

Denhardt, R. B., & Denhardt, J. V. (2000). The new public service: Serving rather than steering. *Public Administration Review, 60*(6), 549–559.

Downs, A. (1957). An economic theory of political action in a democracy. *Journal of Political Economy, 65*(2), 135–150.

Ekman, J., & Amna, E. (2012). Political participation and civic engagement: Towards a new typology. *Human Affairs, 22*, 283–300. doi:10.2478/s13374-012-0024-1.

Falco, E., & Kleinhans, R. (2018). Beyond technology: Identifying local government challenges for using digital platforms for citizen engagement. *International Journal of Information Management, 40*, 17–20. https://doi.org/10.1016/j.ijinfomgt.2018.01.007.

Ganapati, S. (2011). Uses of public participation geographic information systems applications in e-government. *Public Administration Review, 71*(3), 425–434.

Habermas, J. (1992). Further reflections on the public sphere. In Craig Calhoun (Ed.), *Habermas and the public sphere* (pp. 425–451). Cambridge, MA: MIT.

Harmon, M. (1981). *Action theory for public administration*. New York, NY: Longman.

Horlick-Jones, T., Rowe, G., & Walls, J. (2007). Citizen engagement processes as information systems: The role of knowledge and the concept of translation quality. *Public Understanding of Science, 16*(3), 259.

Inglehart, R. (1980). *Culture shift in advanced industrial society*. Princeton, NJ: Princeton University Press.

Innes, J. E., & Booher, D. E. (2004). Reframing public participation: Strategies for the 21st century. *Planning Theory & Practice, 5*(4), 419–436.

Inscape. (2013). A brief history of participation. Retrieved from http://landsc ape.blogspot.com/2013/03/a-brief-history-of-participation.html. Accessed on March 7, 2016.

International Peacebuilding Advisory Team [IPAT]. (2015). Public participation and citizen engagement. Retrieved from www.interpeace.org/wp-content/ uploads/2015/10/2015_10_12_Effective_Advising_How-Public_participa-tion.pdf. Accessed on January 21, 2016.

Irvin, R. A., & Stansbury, J. (2004). Citizen participation in decision making: Is it worth the effort? *Public Administration Review, 64*(1), 55–65.

King, C. S., Feltey, K. M., & Bridget O'Neill, S. (1998). The question of participation: Toward authentic public participation in public administration. *Public Administration Review, 58*(4), 317–327.

Kingston, R., Carver, S., Evans, A., & Turton, I. (2000). Web-based public participation geographical information systems: An aid to local environmental decision-making. *Computers, Environment and Urban Systems, 24*, 109–125.

Le Gales, P. (2011). Policy instruments and governance. In Mark Bevir (Ed.), *The SAGE handbook of governance* (pp. 1–30). London: Sage.

Lee, Y., & Schachter, H. L. (2019). Exploring the relationship between trust in government and citizen participation. *International Journal of Public Administration, 42*(5), 405–416. doi:10.1080/01900692.2018.1465956.

Leighley, J. E. (1995). Attitudes, opportunities and incentives: A field essay on political participation. *Political Research Quarterly, 1*, 181.

Lim, S., & Oh, Y. (2016). Online versus offline participation: Has the democratic potential of the internet been realized? Analysis of a participatory budgeting system in Korea. *Public Performance & Management Review, 39*(3), 676–700.

Lowndes, V., Pratchett, L., & Stoker, G. (2001). Trends in public participation: Part 1 – Local government perspectives. *Public Administration, 79*(1), 205–222.

Lukensmeyer, C. J., & Torres, L. H. (2006). Public deliberation: A manager's guide to citizen engagement. Retrieved from www.whitehouse.gov/files/ documents/ostp/opengov_inbox/ibmpubdelib.pdf. Accessed on January 24, 2016.

McLaverty, P. (2011). Participation. In Mark Bevir (Ed.), *The SAGE handbook of governance* (pp. 1–30). London: Sage.

McSwite, O. (1997). *Legitimacy in public administration a discourse analysis* (Advances in public administration). Thousand Oaks, CA: Sage.

Meijer, A., Burger, N., & Ebbers, W. (2009). Citizens 4 citizens: Mapping participatory practices on the Internet. *Electronic Journal of E-Government, 7*(1), 99–112.

Mergel, I. (2013). A framework for interpreting social media interactions in the public sector. *Government Information Quarterly, 30*, 327–334. http://dx.doi.org/10.1016/j.giq.2013.05.015.

Mettler, S., & Soss, J. (2004). The Consequences of public policy for democratic citizenship: Bridging policy studies and mass politics. *Perspectives on Politics, 2*(1), 55–73. doi:10.1017/S1537592704000623.

Miller, H., & Fox, C. (2007). *Postmodern public administration* (Rev. ed.). Armonk, NY: M.E. Sharpe.

Moehler, D. (2007). Participation in transition: Mobilizing Ugandans in constitution making. *Studies in Comparative International Development, 42*(1/2), 164–190.

Moynihan, D. P. (2003). Normative and instrumental perspectives on public participation: Citizen summits in Washington, DC. *American Review of Public Administration, 33*(2), 164–188.

National Archives. (2016). Administrative Procedure Act. Retrieved from www.archives.gov/federal-register/laws/administrative-procedure/552.html. Accessed on March 5, 2016.

Olson, M. (1965). *The logic of collective action; public goods and the theory of groups*. Cambridge, MA: Harvard University Press.

Parry, G., & Moyser, G. (1994). More participation, more democracy? In D. Beetham (Ed.), *Defining and measuring democracy* (pp. 44–62). London: Sage.

Putnam, R. (2000). *Bowling alone: The collapse and revival of American community*. New York, NY: Simon & Schuster.

Rajani, R. (n.d.). The role of citizen engagement in service delivery. Retrieved from https://d396qusza40orc.cloudfront.net/engagecitizen/pdf/Week%203/Transcript_Rakesh%20Rajani.pdf. Accessed on March 5, 2016.

Rosenstone, S., & Hansen, J. (1993). *Mobilization, participation, and democracy in America*. New York, NY: Macmillan Publishing Company.

Rowe, G., & Frewer, L. J. (2000). Public participation methods: A framework for evaluation. *Science, Technology, and Human Values, 25*(1), 3–29.

Smith, L. G. (1983). *Impact assessment and sustainable resource management*. Harlow: Longman.

Smith, G. (2005). *Beyond the ballot, 57 democratic innovations from around the world*. London: The Power Inquiry.

Thomas, J. C. (1995). *Public participation in public decisions*. San Francisco, CA: Jossey-Bass.

Tolbert, C. J., & Mossberger, K. (2006). The Effects of e-government on trust and confidence in government. *Public Administration Review, 66*(3), 354–369.

United Nations (UN). (2008). The role of active participation and citizen engagement in good governance. Retrieved from www.un.org/esa/socdev/egms/docs/2013/EmpowermentPolicies/Elia%20Armstrong%20presentation.pdf. Accessed on May 7, 2021.

United Nations (UN). (2014). E-government survey 2014. Retrieved from http://unpan3.un.org/egovkb/Portals/egovkb/Documents/un/2014-Survey/E-Gov_Complete_Survey-2014.pdf. Accessed on October 11, 2015.

Van der Arend, S., & Behagel, J. (2011). What participants do? A practice based approach to public participation in two policy fields. *Critical Policy Studies, 5*(2), 169–186.

Verba, S. (1996). The citizen as respondent: Sample surveys and American democracy. *American Political Science Review, 90*, 1–7.

Verba, S., & Nie, N. H. (1972). *Participation in America: Political democracy and social equality*. New York, NY: Harper.

Verba, S., Nie, N. H., & Kim, J. (1978). *Participation and political equality: A seven-nation comparison*. Cambridge: Cambridge University Press.

Verba, S., Schlozman, K., Brady, H., & Nie, N. H. (1993). Citizen activity: Who participates? What do they say? *American Political Science Review, 87*(2), 303–318.

Verba, S., Schlozman, K., & Brady, H. (1995) *Voice and equality: Civic voluntarism in American politics*. Cambridge, MA: Harvard University Press.

Webler, T. (1999). The craft and theory of public participation: A dialectical process. *Journal of Risk Research, 2*(1), 55–71.

3 E-Participation

What Is E-Participation?

Electronic participation, or e-participation, is the use of information and communication technologies (ICTs) to enable citizens to participate in policymaking (UN, 2014). The idea to use ICTs for electronic democracy first emerged in the United States in the early 1970s (Horrocks & Pratchett, 1995). After the growth in popularity of the internet in the 1990s, there was an increase in the awareness that ICTs could be used for wider as well as deeper participation and thus contribute to democratic debate (Macintosh, 2004).

Laudon (1977) identified communication technology forms of three types: data transformation technologies suitable for managerial type of democracy, mass-participation technologies that included opinion polling and interactive cable TV for populist democracy, and interactive technologies (e.g., telephone conference calls) that suit a pluralist model of democracy. Note that the examples are in accordance with the time of the study. It showed that the idea to use communication technology for democratic purposes has been prevalent in technology as well as policy literature even before internet's popularity. Abramson et al. (1988) conducted one of the most comprehensive reviews on effects of a variety of technologies ranging from personal computers, radio, television, to satellites and their relationship to citizen participation, elections, and policymaking (as cited in Ra, 1991). Abramson et al. (1988) further extrapolated the impact of emerging technologies on the future of democracy and identified six important features of ICTs that help define their influence on politics, namely (1) the large volume of information that ICT can manage, (2) information exchange in real time, (3) consumers' control on what messages are received and when (4) senders control on who receives their messages, (5) decentralization of mass communication, and (6) two-way interactive capacity

DOI: 10.4324/9781003164326-3

(as cited in Horrocks & Pratchett, 1995). The advent of the internet was one of the most important developments as it provided a two-way interactivity that made the recipients of information active participants, and this distinguished it from previous mass-participation technologies (Horrocks & Pratchett, 1995). Maturing e-government initiatives, growing awareness for democratic governance, and the public interest in the use of ICT for empowerment of citizens encouraged e-participation initiatives (Phang & Kankanhalli, 2008). The increasing mix of ICTs, low rates of voter turnout, and distrust in political system are some of the other reasons that propelled the idea of e-participation (Horrocks & Pratchett, 1995).

In Chapter 2, the theoretical underpinnings of public participation particularly as grounded in the democracy literature were discussed. E-government and e-participation have been additionally touted in the light of new public management (NPM) and new public service (NPS) (Meijer, 2011; Nabatchi & Mergel, 2010; Torres et al., 2005). The literature on privatization starts with the reform movement around the late 1970s (Kettl, 2015), and NPM strategies started taking shape around the same time (see Denhardt & Denhardt, 2015; and Hood, 1991, for NPM timelines). However, the major work on NPM by Hood (1991) and Osborne and Gaebler (1992), along with Clinton's National Performance Review (NPR), that was aimed at reinventing government to work better and cost less (see Kettl, 2015, for NPR), appeared around the same time as the internet was taking shape in the 1990s. NPM strategies included, among other things, privatization and a strong supporting information technology (IT) systems (Kettl, 2015; West 2005). Privatization and competition in the telecommunications industry is considered critical for healthy competition, innovation, and lowering of ICT prices for consumers (Gulati et al., 2014). However, NPM came under criticism for being an elitist system that viewed citizens as customers and not as democratic participants (e.g., Denhardt & Denhardt, 2000; Dunleavy, 1985; McLaverty, 2011; Pollitt, 1990). Denhardt and Denhardt (2000) proposed principles of NPS as an alternative to NPM. NPS is focused on market-based democratic governance where public service is expected to create opportunities for building citizens' trust, provide citizens the opportunity to define problems for policymaking, and involve citizens in the designing and implementation of solutions (Denhardt & Denhardt, 2000, 2015). Torres et al. (2005) emphasize that e-government aims beyond NPM, as its goal is to transform the relationship between public sector and society.

The early e-government maturity models are influenced with the NPM ideas of technological capability and positivistic rationale in which citizens are treated as customers (Kim & Robinson, 2014). An example is Layne and Lee's (2001) four stages of e-government that begins with cataloguing of documents, online transactions, vertical integration with local systems, and horizontal integration across functions. Similarly, United Nations (UN) and the American Society for Public Administration (ASPA) (2002) proposed a five-stage model of e-government development that starts with establishing an online presence and ends at seamless integration of e-government services. These models have a narrow outlook about the potential of ICT and are comparable to translating e-commerce activities of private sector to the public sector (Torres et al., 2005). The NPS perspective, on the contrary, is citizen-centric instead of customer-centric and promotes a democratic approach. Social media and other information technologies can be used to enhance public participation that can facilitate bottom-up approach. Kim and Robinson (2014), therefore, call for an e-government approach that takes into consideration the expanding public sphere and includes citizens as an essential part of design and practice. They call the approach rooted in NPM a rational design approach, while the NPS-based approach is based on a social design or is a social construction approach (Kim & Robinson, 2014). Later models that discuss stages or levels of e-government (or government's adoption of ICT) often discuss participatory activities as a later stage in e-government. These levels or stages usually begin with the first stage where ICT is used as a one-way communication for information dissemination from the government to the public that later advances to a two-way transaction enabling mechanism; the final stages involve active public participation and empowerment of citizens. As an example, Moon (2002), adapting Hiller and Belanger's (2001) framework, discusses five stages of e-government that are based on the degree of technical sophistication and interaction with users: "(1) simple information dissemination (one-way communication); (2) two-way communication (request and response); (3) service and financial transactions; (4) integration (horizontal and vertical integration); and (5) political participation" (p. 426). Nabatchi and Mergel (2010) adapt a Lukensmeyer and Torres (2006) framework to suggest social media tools along the levels of e-participation that progresses as inform, consult, include/incorporate, collaborate, and empower citizens. The NPS literature claims that online technologies and social media has transformed citizen engagement (Denhardt & Denhardt, 2015; Meijer, 2011; Nabatchi & Mergel, 2010). Nevertheless, Kim and Robinson (2014) argue that there is a lack of connection between the NPS dialogue and e-government model building, and the field of e-government needs to be examined through the NPS point of view.

Why Is E-Participation Important?

E-participation helps to inform citizens of government's actions, identify public needs, educate citizens about policymaking and public issues, utilize public inputs in policymaking, provide opportunities for co-creation of knowledge and of shared and social learning, and enhance accessibility as compared to offline participation through anytime and anywhere information and participatory activities (Phang & Kankanhalli, 2008; Royo et al., 2020). Social media tools such as social networking sites and blogs and mobile apps that are used for informing, sharing, and collaboration have grown exponentially and enable citizens to get involved in policymaking and work with their governments in co-production of services to help governments meet the public needs more responsively and sustainably (Allen et al., 2020; Khan, 2017). Because of the direct two-way communication enabled by the social media, governments can design and execute policy programs that meet the needs of the people (Organization for Economic Co-operation and Development [OECD], 2016).

The state's capacity to redistribute resources and direct their societies has been reduced in the 21st century and governments often face situations where there is no clarity of rules, the outcomes are uncertain, and there may be consequences that are not intended or foreseen. This can lead to increasing participatory governance in the modern states for functional reasons of tapping into local knowledge apart from normative reasons of representative and democratic governance (Smith & Dalakiouridou, 2009). The percentage of countries that have adopted e-participation initiatives in the last two decades is on the rise (Royo et al., 2020). Participation using ICTs reduces transaction and coordination costs, enhances information processing capabilities, and the two-way interaction properties help in better deliberation that improves the quality of policies (Smith & Dalakiouridou, 2009).

Governments that provide opportunities to their citizens to participate in policy decision making and in evaluating government performance generate citizen trust in government (Kim, 2010; Kim & Lee, 2012). Citizen satisfaction with the structure of e-participation processes and applications leads to a more favorable assessment of government transparency and eventually improves trust in government (Kim & Lee, 2012). E-participation, when used for monitoring service performance and providing service feedback, improves service quality, particularly in the case of problems that are complex and involve multiple agencies (Allen et al., 2020).

Concerns and Challenges of E-Participation

There is a tension between technology and the institutional dominance literature. ICTs are considered to have a transformational impact that can change the way government works, make the government accountable and responsive to the citizens, change citizen attitudes, and improve citizen engagement in decision making (Fountain, 2001; Torres et al., 2005; West, 2004). On the other hand, some scholars deny this technological determinism and suggest that IT will not transform democracy but in fact reinforce the existing social and political norms (Chadwick & May, 2003; Davis, 1999; Nam 2012; Norris, 1999).

Some scholars argue that e-participation initiatives generally fail to deliver the various benefits that are expected of it (Royo et al., 2014; Toots, 2019). The citizens are often either not informed of the opportunities to participate and have poor knowledge of the issues or lack sufficient interest for participation (Royo et al., 2014; OECD, 2016). Lack of incentives for public officials to engage citizens in policymaking, lack of awareness about the value added through citizen engagement, and lack of financial and human resources are other main challenges in implementing public participation in policymaking (OECD, 2016; Royo et al., 2014; Viborg et al., 2007). Ignorance about the choice of technology for e-participation, administrative costs involved in e-participation processes, and the complexity of democratic participation make e-participation prone to fail (Toots, 2019; Viborg et al., 2007).

Digital divide, a term that refers to the gap in access to internet and computers, is further linked to power differences in the society that may lead to unequal participation by different sections of the society (Van Dijk, 2006; Warschauer, 2003). The initial digital divide of differences in availability of computers and internet later evolved into differences in ICT skills (Van Deursen & Van Dijk, 2011). As the internet matured and more and more people with lower levels of education started using the internet, the discussion on the digital divide shifted to the differences in the amount and type of usage with some studies suggesting less educated people and women making lesser use of internet news and rural areas using internet for shorter periods of time as compared to urban areas (Van Deursen & Van Dijk, 2014). The digital divide acts as a barrier to realizing effective public participation as it leads to low adoption of ICT tools by certain sections of society and hinders representativeness in policymaking (Royo et al., 2014; Viborg et al., 2007).

Mechanisms of E-Participation

Electronic participation (e-participation) applications include online forums, virtual discussion rooms, electronic juries, and electronic polls (Kim & Lee, 2012). Most governments share policy and budget proposals, legislations, and other related information on their websites, but this is one-way communication. Governments may even provide public kiosks for citizens to access the government information on computer terminals and sometimes distribute storage devices like data storage devices (Chung, 2011). Some governments, on the other hand, have adopted virtual social networks or social media tools like Facebook and Twitter that allow user-generated content creation and sharing of that content, thus enabling two-way communication (Kaplan & Haenlein, 2010; Khan & Krishnan, 2020).

Harechko (2011) divides the mechanisms of e-participation into two groups based on whether the outcomes of the participatory mechanism are (1) mandatory or (2) advisory (recommendations). Mandatory outcomes are generated such as in e-voting or e-elections or e-referendum and e-rulemaking (Harechko, 2011). The advisory outcomes are generated in the case of e-discussions or e-consultation (e.g., online chats, blogs, web forums, and e-polling or e-surveying for informal opinions), in e-initiatives where citizens can engage in agenda setting through forwarding proposals, and in e-petitioning for show of protest or to deliver a recommendation to the government (Harechko, 2011). Other mechanisms include e-representation wherein elected leaders use ICT to enhance their relationship with their constituents that can also be through the development of an e-constituency of those who have similar policy interests (Jackson & Lilleker, 2012). The World e-Parliament Report (Inter-Parliamentary Union [IPU], 2018) details the use of ICTs in legislatures by countries and argues that it has led to a public access to legislative functions by a wider audience and enabled public scrutiny of the legislatures.

Recent publications suggest that the focus of e-participation techniques has moved toward game-based approaches to motivate people to participate by providing experiences similar to games (Bista et al., 2014; Hassan & Hamari, 2019). A recent literature review of the gamification studies suggests that the effects of gamification are positive and that "education, health and crowd sourcing as well as points, badges and leader boards persist as the most common contexts and ways of implementing gamification" (Hassan & Hamari, 2019, p. 191).

Levels of E-Participation

The levels of e-participation refer to how substantially the citizens are engaged in policymaking decisions (Macintosh, 2004). The OECD (2001, 2017) categorizes engagement into three levels of one-way communication of information from the government to citizens, two-way consultation where citizens also provide feedback to government, and active participation where citizens engage in defining the process and content of policymaking. Based on the OECD classification system, Macintosh (2004) developed a three-stage model: (1) e-enabling where technology is used to reach to a wider audience that would not normally use the vast amount of information available online; (2) e-engaging, which refers to deliberating policy issues more deeply and with a wider audience; and (3) e-empowering, where ideas from the citizens influence the political agenda. Similarly, the UN defines a three-level model of e-participation involving e-information, e-consultation, and e-decision making that moves from more passive to active engagement with people (UN, 2014).

UN E-Participation Survey

The UN has been conducting an e-government survey of its member countries since 2001. The effort started through a collaboration between the ASPA and the United Nations Division for Public Economics and Public Administration (UNDPEPA) of the UN Department of Economic and Social Affairs (UNDESA). The intent is to present an objective assessment of the e-government environment in a country and its capacity to sustain online development using a comparative analysis of a country's official online presence, its telecommunications infrastructure, and human capital development for each UN member state (UN and ASPA, 2002). The survey has been conducted for the years 2001 (a benchmarking study), 2003, 2004, 2005, 2008, 2010, 2012, 2014, 2016, 2018, and 2020 by the time when this book is being written. Beginning in 2003, the extent of e-participation is measured as a part of this survey across three stages of e-information, e-consultation, and e-decision making, but the separate scores for the stages are available only since 2014. E-participation seeks to assess the willingness of a country's government to use ICT to provide quality information and effective communication tools for the specific purpose of empowering people for participation, as consumers of public services as well as citizens (UN, 2014). The methodology of assessment includes a review of websites on a quantitative index of items as well as a survey of public sector professionals. The e-participation survey limits itself to exploring only government willingness to promote participation through the use of the ICT and is confined to the citizen-to-government (C2G) and government-to-citizen (G2C) realms (UN, 2014).

As described in Chapter 1, the UN e-Government Survey (UN, 2014) uses a three-level model of e-participation – e-information, e-consultation, and e-decision making – that moves from more passive to active engagement with citizens. The survey looks at all three levels of e-participation across six sectors: education, health, finance, social welfare, labor, and environment. The UN e-government survey measures the facilities for the three levels of participation and not the actual usage.

Mathematically, the e-participation index is normalized by taking the total score value for a given country, subtracting the lowest total score for any country in the UN survey, and dividing by the range of total score values for all countries (UN, 2014). For example, if a country has an e-participation score of x, and the lowest value of any country is 0 and the highest is equal to y, then the e-participation index of that country would be equal to $x - 0/y - 0$. The survey reports the e-participation index, which ranges from 0 to 1 but not the absolute score. The scores for the three stages are reported as a percentage utilization of e-participation across the three stages.

The UN studies recognize the importance of social, political, and economic configurations of a country in its e-government development. At the same time, it recognizes the exceptions as evidenced in its surveys and emphasizes that telecommunications infrastructure, the strength of human capital, political will, and policy and administrative priorities play important roles in e-participation development (UN, 2014).

Factors Impacting E-Participation

Scholars have argued that there is a difference in the resources required for offline and online participation, for example, technology resources such as financial investment in ICTs, knowledge of ICT usage or digital skills, percentage of the population that uses the internet, frequency of internet use, or broadness of the repertoire of internet activities of an individual influences online participation (Anduiza et al., 2010; Gulati et al., 2014; Jho & Song, 2015; Vicente & Novo, 2014). Civic skills that promote the effective navigation of the offline political world may not facilitate online political participation, and individuals may rely instead on new online skills (Best & Krueger, 2005).

At the same time, other scholars argue the importance of institutional resources for e-participation. Enabling institutional factors such as political structure, development of public administrators and appropriate policy initiatives, and democratic institutions are important for e-participation (Chadwick, 2011; Chen & Hsieh, 2009; Gulati et al., 2014; Moon, 2002; Royo et al., 2014; Vicente & Novo, 2014; West, 2005; Zheng et al., 2014). Governments need to develop the required institutional framework for effective e-participation, for example, a central office that oversees all the participatory initiatives and sufficient incentives for citizens to participate and public officials to utilize public participation (OECD, 2016). Institutional arrangements, budget scarcity, group conflict, cultural norms, and prevailing patterns of social and political behavior are constraints on the transformational capabilities of technology (Chen & Hsieh, 2009; Fountain, 2001). Khan and Krishnan (2020) found that quality of national governance and IT governance are both positively associated with e-participation. In their study, the national governance refers to the indicators such as voice and accountability, rule of law, political stability, and regulatory quality as measured by the Kauffman index (Kaufmann et al., 1999), and IT governance refers to the government's utilization of ICT for competitiveness as measured by the World Economic Forum (Khan & Krishnan, 2020). Apart from these, socioeconomic factors of age, gender, education, and employment status and locality characteristics of municipality or city size and population are also found to be significant predictors of e-participation (Leigh & Atkinson; 2001; Norris, 2001; Norris & Reddick, 2013; Novo Vázquez & Vicente, 2019).

A few studies have conducted cross-national analyses of the nature that the current study is interested in undertaking (e.g., Åström et al., 2012; Gulati et al., 2014; Jho & Song, 2015; Zhao et al., 2014). All these studies use the UN e-participation survey results as a measure for their dependent variable. Åström et al. (2012) study the impact of domestic and international factors on e-participation where the international factor is globalization. Gulati et al. (2014) study the impact of governance on online services and e-participation. Zhao et al. (2014) study national culture as the predictor of e-government diffusion with economic development as the moderator. Jho and Song (2015) study the impact of technology, institutions, and their interactions on civic e-participation. The theories used in the four studies are (1) Åström et al. (2012) use the Washington hypothesis of economic globalization that argues societies will open up as the development of capital markets prevents rent-seeking activities and increase the bargaining power of businesses (Maxfield, 1998; Rudra, 2005), (2) Gulati et al. (2014) refer to Fountain's (2001) theoretical framework, (3) Jho and Song (2015) do not cite any particular theory as the basis for their analytical model, and (4) Zhao et al. (2014) use contingency theories that emphasize the importance of the effects of environment (contingency factors) on performance. Table 3.1 lists exclusively these four studies that have used quantitative data with statistical analysis in a cross-country comparison

Table 3.1 Factors in e-participation cross-national studies

Study	Dependent variable/s	Explanatory variables	Measures and data sources
Jho and Song (2015)	Civil e-Participation Source: UN E-participation Index (2012)	Political institutions	Political rights and civil liberties – level of institutionalization of freedom of speech and association – Freedom House, 2012 Level of democracy – Economic Intelligence Unit (EIU)
		Technology	Online population–%individuals usinginternet–International Telecommunication Union (ITU, 2012)
		Moderating effects between technology and institutions	
		Control variable: socioeconomic	HDI – UNDP, 2013 – this index incorporates actual national income, level of education, rate of illiteracy, and average citizen lifespan
Åström, Karlsson et al. (2012)	E-participation index Source: UN e-participation survey	Domestic factors: technological development, democracy development	Technological development – the spread of internet use – internet users per 100 people – ITU democratization – a combined Freedom House/Polity measure of democratization levels of development and modernization – HDI – UNDP

(*continued*)

Table 3.1 Cont.

Study	Dependent variable/s	Explanatory variables	Measures and data sources
		International factor–economic globalization	KOF Index of Globalization
Gulati et al. (2014)	Online services and e-participation Measures: (1) online service index (2) e-participation index Source: UN's E-government and E-participation index	Investment	Gulati and Yates' (2011) Financial Investment Index to measure a nation's financial investment in ICTs
		Competition	Gulati and Yates' (2011) Telecommunications Competition Index
		Governance	Worldwide Governance Indicators (WGI) project – (1) government effectiveness, (2) regulatory quality, (3) rule of law, (4) political stability and absence of violence, (5) control of corruption, and (6) voice and accountability
		Control variables: democratic politics urbanization land area education	Democratic politics – Unified Democracy Scores (UDS) for 2008 (the UDS is derived from ten frequently used indicators of democracy, e.g., Polity IV and Freedom House to produce a single composite scale). Urbanization –

Table 3.1 Cont.

Study	Dependent variable/s	Explanatory variables	Measures and data sources
			percentage of residents living in urban areas – CIA website, 2011 Land area – country's total size in square kilometers – CIA website, 2011 Education – UN Education Index
Zhao et al. (2014)	E-government diffusion Measures: UN's survey (1) E-government development index (2) E-participation index	National culture	GLOBE by House et al. (2004) – (1) uncertainty avoidance, (2) power distance, (3) in-group collectivism, (4) future orientation, and (5) performance orientation
		Economic development as moderating variable	Gross national income (GNI) per capita – World Bank

Source: Author's own compilation of e-participation cross-national literature.

across the world. The explanatory variables used in these studies along with their measures and data sources are listed in the table. These studies use e-participation index of UN survey as their dependent variable and most closely represent the type of effort that the current study is undertaking. These studies also provide the basis for gap analysis in the literature.

Gaps in the Literature

Several gaps are identified in the cross-country quantitative studies. One main gap is the missing path analysis about the effect of various technology and institutional variables on e-participation in cross-national studies. The studies either explore the simultaneous impact of these variables or, at most, the moderator effect of a variable. The current study aims to address this gap by studying direct and indirect effects of technology and institutional variables on e-participation.

Second, the variables and measures whose impact on e-participation has been studied in cross-national studies are very limited. The only technology measure studied as a predictor is percentage of individuals using the internet (in Jho & Song, 2015; and Åström et al., 2012). Clearly, a large number of variables and measures are yet to be studied in cross-national online participation, when compared to offline participation studies and other e-government and ICT adoption studies. The impact of important technology features such as ICT usage, and ICT affordability on e-participation is not assessed.

Third, the use of composite indices, in some cases, fails to provide a focused area of public policy for action. For example, the Human Development Index (HDI) is a composite index that includes national income, level of education, rate of illiteracy, and average citizen lifespan. Using this index as a measure of development or modernization (Åström et al., 2012) or socioeconomic condition (Jho & Song, 2015) denies one information about the independent impact of income or education on e-participation. More appropriate measures can be used for analysis, for example, as a measure for their control variable of education, Gulati et al. (2014) use the UN education index 2007/2008 (UN, 2007) that assesses enrollment in secondary or tertiary education, although a more focused predictor for online skills can be the World Economic Forum's skill index that is based on quality of educational system and math and science education along with enrollment.

Another gap is that the impact of interaction between technology and institutions on e-participation is underutilized with just one study (i.e., Jho & Song, 2015) analyzing moderating effects with a single technology variable. The current study uses multiple dimensions of technology and institutions to draw attention toward the argument that neither technology nor institution independently influence e-participation. Moreover, the important aspect of the digital divide is minimally attended to and rarely discussed in the existing cross-national studies. As discussed earlier, under the section on concerns and challenges of e-participation, the focus in the definition of digital divide moved from a gap in access to computers and the internet to ICT skills and then to ICT usage. The digital divide is paid diligent attention in this study through the multiple dimensions used for the explanatory variables of technology to assess the digital divide and its impact on e-participation. Chapter 4 discusses the literature in the policy feedback theory and theories of socio-technical premises to develop a conceptual framework for cross-country analysis of e-participation.

References

Abramson, J. B., Arterton, F. C., & Orren, G. R. (1988). *The electronic commonwealth: The impact of new media technologies on democratic politics.* New York, NY: Basic Books.

Allen, B., Tamindael, L. E., Bickerton, S. H., Cho., W. (2020). Does citizen coproduction lead to better urban services in smart cities projects? An empirical study on e-participation in a mobile big data platform. *Government Information Quarterly, 37*(1), 1–10.

Anduiza, E., Gallego, A., & Cantijoch, M. (2010). Online political participation in Spain: The impact of traditional and internet resources. *Journal of Information Technology & Politics, 7*(4), 356–368.

Åström, J., Karlsson, M., Linde, J., & Pirannejad, A. (2012). Understanding the rise of e-participation in non-democracies: Domestic and international factors. *Government Information Quarterly, 29*(2), 142–150.

Best, S., & Krueger, J. (2005). Analyzing the representativeness of internet political participation. *Political Behavior, 27*(2), 183–216.

Bista, S. K., Nepal, S., Paris, C., & Colineau, N. (2014). Gamification for online communities: A case study for delivering government services. *International Journal of Cooperative Information Systems, 23*(2), 1441002-1–1441002-25.

Chadwick, A. (2011). Explaining the failure of an online citizen engagement initiative: The role of internal institutional variables. *Journal of Information Technology & Politics, 8*(1), 21–40.

Chadwick, A., & May, C. (2003). Interaction between states and citizens in the age of the Internet: "E-government" in the United States, Britain, and the European Union. *Governance: An International Journal of Policy, Administration and Institutions, 16* (2), 271–300.

Chen, Y., & Hsieh, J. (2009). Advancing e-governance: Comparing Taiwan and the United States. *Public Administration Review, 69*(S1), S151–S158. doi:10.1111/j.1540-6210.2009.02103.x.

Chung, S. Y. (2011). Fostering citizen participation though innovative mechanisms in governance, policy, and decision making: Comparing Washington, DC and Seoul. Retrieved from https://repository.asu.edu/attachments/56573/content/Chung_asu_0010E_10526.pdf. Accessed on November 9, 2020.

Davis, R. (1999). *The web of politics: The internet's impact on the American political system.* New York, NY: Oxford University Press.

Denhardt, J. V., & Denhardt, R. B. (2015). The new public service revisited. *Public Administration Review, 75*(5), 664–672.

Denhardt, R. B., & Denhardt, J. V. (2000). The new public service: serving rather than steering. *Public Administration Review, 60*(6), 549–559. Dunleavy, P. J. (1985). Bureaucrats, budgets and the growth of the state. *British Journal of Political Science, 15*, 299–328.

Fountain, J. (2001). *Building the virtual state information technology and institutional change.* Washington, DC: Brookings Institution Press.

Freedom House. (2012). Freedom in the world 2012. Retrieved 3rd June 2021 from https://freedomhouse.org/report/freedom-world/freedom-world-2012.

Gulati, G., Williams, C. B., & Yates, D. J. (2014). Predictors of on-line services and e-participation: A cross-national comparison. *Government Information Quarterly, 3*(1), 526–533. doi:10.1016/j.giq.2014.07.005.

Gulati, G. J., & Yates, D. J. (2011). Strategy, competition, and investment: Explaining the global divide in e-government implementation with policy variables. *Electronic Government: An International Journal, 8*(2/3), 124–143.

Harechko, I. (2011). Basic mechanisms of e-participation of citizens in policy-making. *Toruńskie Studia Międzynarodowe, 1/2011*(4), 21–32.

Hassan, L., & Hamari, J. (2019). Gamification of e-participation: A literature review. Proceedings of the 52nd Hawaii International Conference on System Sciences. doi:10.24251/HICSS.2019.372. Retrieved from http://hdl.handle.net/10125/59744. Accessed on November 4, 2020.

Hiller, J., & Belanger, F. (2001). Privacy strategies for electronic government. E-Government Series. Arlington, VA: PricewaterhouseCoopers Endowment for the Business of Government.

Hood, C. (1991). A public management for all seasons? *Public Administration, 69*(1), 3–19.

Horrocks, I., & Pratchett, L. (1995). Electronic democracy: Central themes and issues. In J. Lovenduski & J. Stanyer (Eds.), *Contemporary political studies 1995: Proceedings of the annual conference of the political studies association of the UK, volume 3* (pp. 1218–1226). Belfast: Political Studies Association. Retrieved from www.clubofamsterdam.com/contentarticles/Democracy%20and%20New%20Technology.pdf. Accessed on November 3, 2020.

House, R. J., Hanges, P. J., Javidan, M., Dorfman, P. W., & Gupta, V. (Eds.). (2004). *Culture, leadership, and organizations: The GLOBE study of 62 societies*. London: Sage publications.

Inter-Parliamentary Union (IPU). (2018). Preparation of the world e-parliament report 2018. Retrieved from www.ipu.org/work-with-ipu/vacancies/2017-04/preparation-world-e-parliament-report-2018. Accessed on November 9, 2020.

International Telecommunication Union (ITU). (2020). Measuring digital development: Facts and figures, 2020. Retrieved 16th February 2021 from www.itu.int/en/ITU-D/Statistics/Documents/facts/FactsFigures2020.pdf.

Jackson, N., & Lilleker, D. G. (2012). The member for cyberspace: E-representation and MPs in the UK. In A. Prerna & S. Braga (Eds.), *E-parliament and ICT-based legislation: Concept, experiences and lessons* (pp. 64–79). Hershey: IGI Global.

Jho, W., & Song, K. J. (2015). Institutional and technological determinants of civil e-participation: Solo or duet? *Government Information Quarterly, 3*(2), 488–495. doi:10.1016/j.giq.2015.09.003.

Kaplan, A. M., & Haenlein, M. (2010). Users of the world, unite! The challenges and opportunities of Social Media. *Business Horizons, 53*(1), 59–68.

Kaufmann, D., Kray, A., & Zoido-Lobotan, P. (1999). *Governance matters (policy research working paper 2196)*. Washington, DC: The World Bank Development Research Group.

Kettl, D. F. (2015). Governing in an age of transformation. In J. L. Perry & R. K. Christensen (Eds.), *Handbook of public administration* (3rd ed.). San Francisco: Jossey-Bass, pp. 5–22.

Khan, A., & Krishnan, S. (2020). Virtual social networks diffusion, governance mechanisms, and e-participation implementation: A cross-country investigation. *E-Service Journal, 11*(3), 36–69. doi:10.2979/eservicej.11.3.02.

Khan, G .F. (2017). *Social media for government: A practical guide to understanding, implementing, and managing social media tools in the public sphere*. Singapore: Springer.

Kim, B. J. & Robinson, S. (2014). In E. Downey & M. A. Jones (Eds.), *Public service, governance and Web 2.0 technologies: Future trends in social media.* Hershey: IGI Global.

Kim, S. (2010). Public trust in government in Japan and South Korea: Does the rise of critical citizens matter? *Public Administration Review, 70*(5), 801–810.

Kim, S., & Lee, J. (2012). E-participation, transparency, and trust in local government. *Public Administration Review, 72*(6), 819–828. https://doi-org.proxy.lib.odu.edu/10.1111/j.1540-6210.2012.02593.x.

Laudon, K. (1977). *Communications technology and democratic participation* (Praeger special studies in US economic, social, and political issues). New York, NY: Praeger.

Layne, & Lee. (2001). Developing fully functional e-government: A four stage model. *Government Information Quarterly, 18*(2), 122–136.

Leigh, A., & Atkinson, R. (2001). *Clear thinking on the digital divide.* Washington, DC: Progressive Policy Institute.

Lukensmeyer, C. J., & Torres, L. H. (2006). Public deliberation: A manager's guide to citizen engagement. Retrieved from www.whitehouse.gov/files/documents/ostp/opengov_inbox/ibmpubdelib.pdf. Accessed on January 24, 2016.

Macintosh, A. (2004). Characterizing e-participation in policy-making. Proceedings of the, Big Island, HI, 2004, 37th Annual Hawaii International Conference on System Sciences, June 2004. doi:10.1109/HICSS.2004.1265300.

Maxfield, S. (1998). Effects of international portfolio flows on government policy choice. In M. Kahler (Ed.), *Capital flows and financial crises* (pp. 69–92). Manchester: Manchester University Press.

McLaverty, P. (2011). Participation. In Mark Bevir (Ed.), *The SAGE handbook of governance* (pp. 1–30). London: Sage.

Meijer, A. J. (2011). Networked coproduction of public services in virtual communities: From a government-centric to a community approach to public service support. *Public Administration Review, 71*(4), 598–607.

Moon, M. (2002). The evolution of e-government among municipalities: Rhetoric or reality? *Public Administration Review, 62*(4), 424–433. doi:10.1111/0033-3352.00196.

Nabatchi, T., & Mergel, I. (2010). Participation 2.0: Using Internet and social media technologies to promote distributed democracy and create digital neighborhoods. In J. H. Svara & J. Denhardt (Eds.), *Connected communities: Local governments as a partner in citizen engagement and community building* (pp. 80–87). Phoenix, AZ: Alliance for Innovation.

Nam, T. (2012). Dual effects of the internet on political activism: Reinforcing and mobilizing. *Government Information Quarterly, 29*(S1), S90–S97.

Norris, D. F., & Reddick, C. G. (2013). Local e-government in the United States: Transformation or incremental change? *Public Administration Review, 73*(1), 165–175.

Norris, P. (1999). Who surfs? New technology, old voters and virtual democracy in the 1996 and 1998 US elections. Paper presented at the American Political Science Association conference, Atlanta, GA.

Norris, P. (2001). *Digital divide: Civic engagement, information poverty, and the internet worldwide.* Cambridge: Cambridge University Press.

Novo Vázquez, A., & Vicente, M. R. (2019). Exploring the determinants of e-participation in smart cities. Public Administration and Information Technology. In M. P. R. Bolívar & L. A. Muñoz (Eds.), *E-participation in smart cities: Technologies and models of governance for citizen engagement* (pp. 157–178). Cham: Springer. https://doi.org/10.1007/978-3-319-89474-4_8.

Organization for Economic Co-operation and Development (OECD). (2001). Citizens as partners: Information, consultation and public participation in policymaking: OECD. Retrieved from www.oecd.org/gov/digital-government/2536857.pdf. Accessed on November 4, 2020.

Organization for Economic Co-operation and Development (OECD). (2016). Open government: The global context and the way forward. Retrieved from www.oecd.org/publications/open-government-9789264268104-en.htm. Accessed on November 5, 2020.

Organization for Economic Co-operation and Development (OECD). (2017). Recommendation of the council on open government. OECD/LEGAL/0438 Adopted on 13/12/2017. Retrieved from https://legalinstruments.oecd.org/en/instruments/OECD-LEGAL-0438. Accessed on November 4, 2020.

Osborne, D., & Gaebler, T. (1992). *Reinventing government: How the entrepreneurial spirit is transforming the public sector.* New York, NY: Plenum.

Phang, C. W., & Kankanhalli, A. (2008). A framework of ICT exploitation for e-participation initiatives. *Communications of the ACM, 51*(12), 128. https://doi.org/10.1145/1409360.1409385.

Pollitt, C. (1990). *Managerialism and the public services: The Anglo-American experience.* Oxford: Blackwell.

Ra, J. O. (1991). American politics. Review of the book *The electronic commonwealth: The impact of new media technologies on democratic politics* by J. B. Abramson, F. C. Arterton, & G. R. Orren. *American Political Science Review, 85*(1), 291.

Royo, S., Vicente, P., & Jaime, G. R. (2020). Decide Madrid: A critical analysis of an award-winning e-participation initiative. *Sustainability, 12*(4), 1–19.

Royo, S., Yetano, A., Acerete, B. (2014). E-participation and environmental protection: Are local governments really committed? *Public Administration Review, 74*, 87–98.

Rudra, N. (2005). Globalization and the strengthening of democracy in the developing world. *American Journal of Political Science, 49*(4), 704–730.

Smith, S., & Dalakiouridou, E. (2009). Contextualising public (e)participation in the governance of the European Union. *European Journal of ePractice, 7*(March 2009), 1–11.

Toots, M. (2019). Why e-participation systems fail: The case of Estonia's Osale. ee. *Government Information Quarterly, 36*(3), 546–559.

Torres, L., Pina, V., & Royo, S. (2005). E-government and the transformation of public administrations in EU countries: Beyond NPM or just a second wave of reforms? *Online Information Review, 29*(5), 531–553.

United Nations. (2007). Human development report 2007/2008. Retrieved from http://hdr.undp.org/sites/default/files/reports/268/hdr_20072008_en_compl ete.pdf. Accessed on June 30, 2017.

United Nations. 2013. Human Development Report 2013. Available at http://hdr.undp.org/sites/default/files/reports/14/hdr2013_en_complete.pdf.

United Nations. (2014). E-government survey 2014. Retrieved from http://unp an3.un.org/egovkb/Portals/egovkb/Documents/un/2014-Survey/E-Gov_ Complete_Survey-2014.pdf. Accessed on October 11, 2015.

United Nations, & American Society for Public Administration. (2002). *Benchmarking e-government: A global perspective.* New York, NY: U.N. Publications.

Van Deursen, A. J., & Van Dijk, J. (2011). Internet skills and the digital divide. *New Media & Society, 13*(6), 893–911. https://doi.org/10.1177/146144481 0386774.

Van Deursen, A. J., & Van Dijk, J. A. (2014). The digital divide shifts to differences in usage. *New Media & Society, 16*(3), 507–526. https://doi.org/ 10.1177/1461444813487959.

Van Dijk, J. A. G. M. (2006, August–October). Digital divide research, achievements and shortcomings. *Poetics, 34* (4–5), 221–235.

Viborg, A., Zinner, K., Henriksen, H., Secher, C., & Medaglia, R. (2007). Costs of e-participation: The management challenges. *Transforming Government: People, Process and Policy, 1*(1), 29–43. https://doi.org/10.1108/1750616071 0733689.

Vicente, M. R., & Novo, A. (2014). An empirical analysis of e-participation. The role of social networks and e-government over citizens' online engagement. *Government Information Quarterly, 31*(3), 379–387.

Warschauer, M. (2003). *Technology and social inclusion: Rethinking the digital divide.* Cambridge and London: MIT Press.

West, D. M. (2004). E-government and the transformation of service delivery and citizen attitudes. *Public Administration Review, 1*, 15.

West, D. M. (2005). *Digital government technology and public sector performance* (Safari tech books online ed.). Princeton, NJ: Princeton University Press.

Zhao, F., Shen, K., & Collier, A. (2014). Effects of national culture on e-government diffusion – A global study of 55 countries. *Information & Management, 51*(8), 1005–1016.

Zheng, Y., Schachter, H. L., & Holzer, M. (2014). The impact of government form on e-participation: A study of New Jersey municipalities. *Government Information Quarterly, 3*(1), 653–659.

4 A Framework for Analyzing E-Participation

Overview

The literature informs a range of factors that impact e-participation. Factors prominent in the combined offline and online participation literature that are relevant for the current e-participation study are combined in this study into two main categories: the institutional factors such as democratic institutions, regulatory quality, and quality of governance (Chen & Hsieh, 2009; Fountain, 2001; Putnam, 2000; Verba, 1996; West, 2005; Zhao et al., 2014); and the technological factors, where technology refers to the information and communication technology (ICT) (Chen & Hsieh, 2009; Gulati et al., 2014; Jho & Song, 2015). These are the two set of predictors that are explored for their influence on e-participation in the current research. A third set of factors are in the demographic and socioeconomic category. Factors in this third set are used as control variables in this study. The theoretical frameworks that inform this study are (1) policy feedback theory (Mettler, 2002; Mettler & Sorrelle, 2018; Mettler & Soss, 2004; Pierson, 1993); (2) structuration theory (Giddens, 1984); and (3) its extension, technology-in-practice (Orlikowski, 2000). Orlikowski's (2000) work is based on Giddens' (1984) structuration theory, and both these works fall under the broader category of socio-technical approaches. The discussion of theories is followed by development of hypothesis through a discussion of evidence in existing literature. Figures are used at the end of each subsection to represent the step-by-step development of the framework. A comprehensive conceptual framework for the current study is illustrated at the end of this chapter along with a list of hypotheses, variables, and data sources.

DOI: 10.4324/9781003164326-4

Policy Feedback Theory

Schattschneider (1935) was the first to argue that policies shape new interests, constituencies, and future politics (Hacker & Pierson, 2014). Lowi (1972) categorized policies based on similar argument as he theorized that different types of policies exist, and each policy type determines a different pattern of politics. Scholars began to explore how an enacted policy restructures subsequent political processes, and several studies supported this notion that policies have a feedback effect that impacts future politics (e.g., Campbell, 2003; Patashnik, 2008; Pierson, 1994). Skocpol (1992) proposed the apt term of "policy feedback" for this literature (Mettler & Sorrelle, 2018).

Policy feedback theory assesses the impact of policies and programs on governance and future policy creation (Mettler & Sorrelle, 2018; Mettler & Welsch, 2004). It argues that policies are political forces that can facilitate or restrain institutional capacity to pursue initiatives and shape positions and interests (Moynihan & Soss, 2014). Pierson (1993, p. 595) explains that in policy feedback, the "effect becomes cause," where the outcomes of the previous policies impact future policy developments by creating resources and interpretive effects. Thus, drawing from Pierson's (1993) argument, for public participation, the public policies engender: (1) resource effects that provide the capacity to participate, and (2) interpretive effects that influence the perceptions of the individuals about their role in the society and government (Campbell, 2012; Mettler, 2002; Moynihan & Soss, 2004). Pierson's (1993) policy feedback theory is used by scholars to assess public participation (Mettler & Sorrelle, 2018). Mettler and Soss (2004, p. 55), for example, use policy feedback to explain how policies influence mass politics by "structuring, stimulating, and stalling political participation." Similarly, others argue that even the interactions of the citizens with public administrators are shaped by public policies that in turn affect citizens' political views on issues such as civic standing, rights, and power (Moynihan & Soss, 2014; Soss et al., 2011). Policies influence citizen participation by "affecting levels of politically relevant resources, affecting feelings of political engagement such as political efficacy and political interest, and affecting the likelihood of political mobilization by interest groups and other political entrepreneurs" (Campbell, 2012, p. 336).

The participation literature, both offline and online, credits the "resources approach" as the most popular explanation for citizen's social and political participation (Anduizo et al., 2010; Vicente & Novo, 2014). The resource approach emphasizes that social and political participation requires resources such as time, money, and other factors (Vicente & Novo, 2014). This approach contrasts with prior theories that suggested that deprivation and grievances explain social and political engagement (Vicente & Novo, 2014). While the work by Mettler (2002) and others (Mettler & Sorrelle, 2018; Mettler & Soss 2004) cite Pearson's policy feedback theory when talking about the resources effect, other studies under the resources approach do not mention Pierson (1993) or policy feedback effects (e.g., Anduizo et al., 2010; Vicente & Novo, 2014). For example, Vicente and Novo (2014) categorize all requirements such as individual and group resources, and institutional and political environments as resources for political participation, and their work does not particularly refer to Pierson's (1993) policy feedback theory.

However, the literature cited in both the policy feedback-based mass-participation approach and the resources approach are the same; for example, Verba et al.'s (1995) civic voluntarism model or the work of Lazarsfeld et al. (1948) are cited in both bodies of work. Mettler (2002) combined Pierson's (1993) work with the learnings from Verba et al.'s (1995) civic voluntarism model to make the former applicable to civic engagement. Vicente and Novo (2014), on the other hand, cite Verba et al.'s (1995) work in developing categories of resources that help explain social and political participation. Vicente and Novo (2014) identify four types of resources in the participation literature: (1) individual resources or the socioeconomic characteristics such as age, gender, education level, and income (e.g., Norris, 2001; Verba, 1996; Verba et al., 1995), although some recent literature shows that the poor are no less interested in democratic participation (Krishna, 2008); (2) political attitudes such as personal efficacy or political interest (Verba et al., 1978); (3) group resources such as a network of friends (Putnam, 2000); and (4) institutional and political environments that affect individual attitudes, such as trust, that further affects participation (Eisinger, 1973). The traditional (e.g., Lazarsfeld et al., 1948) and more contemporary literature (e.g., Norris, 2001) rely on the resources approach (Vicente & Novo, 2014). McCarthy and Zald (2001) discuss the resources approach as resource mobilization theory that was developed to understand collective action and social movements and argue that this approach started developing around the 1970s. Mettler and Soss (2004) conclude that there is a diverse literature in the field with few realizing that it has a common thread. They criticize the extant literature by pointing out that policy effects are generally analyzed as social or economic outcomes, and their impact on democratic practices has been of less concern to scholars (Mettler & Soss, 2004). Verba et al.'s (1995) civic voluntarism model applied to offline participation is a seminal model underlining resources effect. It argues that people with more money, time, and skills are more likely to participate (Anduizo et al., 2010).

In the online participation world, the resources model argues two things: First, the traditional resources can shape the online participation, and second, new resources of ICT and computer skills are required (Anduizo et al., 2010). On one hand, scholars argue that people with the traditional resources such as higher levels of education and income are more likely to use the internet (e.g., Norris, 2001). On the other hand, scholars argue that the resources required for online participation are different; traditional resources such as time are less important for online participation (e.g., Best & Krueger, 2005; Krueger, 2002) and increasing internet skills enable online participation (Krueger, 2002). After the advent of the internet, its effect on participation, based on the resources approach, has been the subject interest of several studies (Anduizo et al., 2010; Best & Krueger, 2005; Hansen & Reinau, 2006; Krueger, 2002; Norris, 2001; Vicente & Novo, 2014), and internet connections and digital skills are studied and identified as key resources to explain e-participation (Anduizo et al., 2010; Krueger, 2002; Vicente & Novo, 2014).

The takeaway from the foregoing discussion on policy feedback theory is its agreement that participation requires resources, and that existing government policies provide or constrain those resources. The resources can be physical resources or people's interpretations of the existing rules and regulations, and these together shape the future citizen engagement. This theory helps develop the basic analytical framework for the current study. In the current study, resources for participation are identified based on the literature review and are used as the explanatory (and control) factors for e-participation. In this study, two categories of resources are included as explanatory variables: (1) technological resources that enable the citizens in a country to participate in political activities online, and (2) the institutional resources that facilitate the availability and usage of the technical resources by citizens for participation and also shape citizens' interpretation of their role in the society that influences their behavior toward citizen engagement.

Socio-Technical Theories

The previous section discussed the policy feedback theory and its resource and interpretive effects. This section discusses the theories under the socio-technical premises to develop a more nuanced understanding of how the technological and institutional resources affect e-participation. To include the interaction effects of technology and institutions and the impact of usage of technology on e-participation, this study depends on the theories under the socio-technical premises.

Trist et al. (1963) introduced the term "socio-technical" first as a result of observations made in an action-research project by Tavistock Institute of Human Relations in the British coal-mining industry. Their argument was that organizations need not conform to the Tayloristic (Taylor, 1967) and bureaucratic principles as social and technical systems can no longer be viewed as separate approaches (Trist, 1981). Work in organizations requires people to use technology, and work organizations are socio-technical systems that require worker participation (Trist, 1981, 1989). Socio-technical systems consist of "... artefacts, knowledge, capital, labor, cultural meaning, etc." (Geels, 2004, p. 900). Approaches such as actor–network theory (Callon & Law, 1989; Latour, 1987) emphasize that institutions and rules coordinate (but do not determine) human actions, and technologies and material contexts such as buildings, roads, elevators, appliances, and so on shape human perceptions and behavior (Geels, 2004). Socio-technical systems thus form a structuring context for human action (Geels, 2004). Three analytic dimensions – systems, actors, and rules – are identified (Geels, 2004). Dynamic interactions take place between these three, and human activities are either viewed as forces of change (agency) or those following iron rules (structure) (Geels, 2004). Approaches such as that of Giddens' (1984) theory of structuration attempt to solve the structure agency dilemma (Geels, 2004). Giddens' (1984) theory of structuration argues that behavior and structure are intertwined – social structures shape human activities and, in turn, are shaped by those activities. Structure is the influence or constraint in the form of rules and resources on individual or group actions (Giddens, 1984). Several approaches have developed under the socio-technical premise, some of which are intertwined with the Tavistock work (Trist et al., 1963) and others that are independent of it (Sawyer & Jarrahi, 2013).

The socio-technical approach recognizes that technology systems and social norms such as rules of use and participation by a broad range of human stakeholders are inextricably intertwined; that they both have the ability to act, and that this interaction is not independent of surrounding events resulting in co-evolution (Sawyer & Jarrahi, 2013). Contextual factors such as social structures shape the interaction between human and technology (Sawyer, 2006). Socio-technical research is based on the interdependent and intertwined relationships between technological object or system and the social norms (Sawyer & Jarrahi, 2013). The technical system focuses on the processes, tasks, and technologies to produce designated output, and the social system on attributes such as people's relationships, rules, attitudes, and values (Bostrom & Heinen, 1977a, 1977b).

The socio-technical approaches do not seek a single dominant cause of change like the socially or technologically deterministic views (Callon & Law 1989; Latour, 1987; Sawyer & Jarrahi, 2013). In the socio-technical premise, ICT is embedded in the social context that both adapts to and helps reshape the social world through design, development, deployment, and use (Avgerou, 2001; Kling, 1980; Orlikowski, 1992; Sawyer & Jarrahi, 2013). Institutions, people, and technological artifacts together influence adoption and uses of any information system (Kling et al., 2003). Fountain's (2001) technology enactment framework examines how institutions influence the way a system is used by the actors. Institutional influences, such as organizational structures including behaviors and norms, governmental rules and laws, cultural institutions, and bureaucracy, each play a role and are interrelated in their influence on technology enactment (Fountain, 2001). The technology enactment framework divides technology into "objective" technology, that refers to the material systems like hardware and software, and "enacted" technology that refers to design, implementation, and how technology is used in an organization (Fountain, 2006, p. 6). The enacted technology is impacted by the organizational forms and institutional arrangements but at the same time both objective and enacted technology also influence the form and culture of the organization. The outcomes of this socio-technical system further influence the technology and institutions in her framework.

Socio-technical approaches are profusely utilized in information technology (IT) studies. In a participation behavior study of users in a Web 2.0 environment, Chai and Kim (2012) use socio-technical approach to help understand the way in which technology is adopted and used in an organization. E-government studies cite one or more socio-technical works (e.g., Fountain, 2001; Giddens, 1984; Kling & Lamb, 2000; Orlikowski, 1992, 2000; Orlikowski & Iacono, 2001) and argue that e-government is a complex and multifaceted phenomenon that requires the knowledge of both the e-government project and its context (e.g., Bwalya et al., 2014; Gil-Garcia, 2012; Gil-Garcia & Pardo, 2006). The technology enactment framework (Fountain, 2001) is based on the premise that it is the interaction between technology and institutions that influences adoption and enactment of technology. Structuration theory (Giddens, 1984; Orlikowski, 1992, 2000) is used to study the relations between ICTs and the organizational and interorganizational structures for adoption of e-democracy by elected members (Parvez, 2008). It is also used to make sense of how the social structures influence actors in shaping e-democracy, and the role e-democracy plays in the democratic process (Parvez, 2006). Giddens' (1984) structuration theory is used to understand how the interactions between actors shapes and modifies institutionalized social structures leading to a mutual reshaping of government-led and citizen-led e-participation (Porwol et al., 2013). Studies based on this theory have found that technology-oriented thinking has constrained the deployment of e-government by local authorities (Senyucel, 2007). An Absence of norms or guidance on what to do (or not to do) and the absence of formal rules leads to tensions between users and providers, constraining deployment, and usage (Senyucel, 2007). Using the socio-technical approach in e-government, scholars suggest that governments need to look beyond technology and into organizational, political, cultural, and required resources for e-government success (Gil-Garcia & Pardo, 2006; Weerakkody et al., 2007).

Structuration theory and its applications by other scholars (Fountain, 2001; Giddens, 1984; Orlikowski, 1992, 2000) inform the current study as they bring out the intertwined nature of social and technical systems and the role of usage of technology, or technology enactment, in shaping behavior. Structuration approach examines the social and organizational structures and their relationship with information technologies (Gil-Garcia, 2012). The current study assumes that neither technology nor institutions work independently for encouraging e-participation, but it is their interaction, their shaping of each other, that affects e-participation. This study attempts to determine how technology and institutions both shape e-participation by examining the moderating and mediating impacts of each on the other.

Technology Resources

Physical resources of ICT are a must for e-participation. Most of the previous cross-country e-participation studies have focused only on one narrow measure of technology: the availability of internet connections as a percentage of population (e.g., Jho & Song, 2015). The current study focuses on four dimensions of ICT as predictors for e-participation: infrastructure, affordability, skills, and usage.

ICT Infrastructure

ICT infrastructure ensures availability of a basic platform for citizens to interact online with their government. Physical access to ICT infrastructure is still a critical need, especially for the least developed countries

(International Telecommunication Union [ITU], 2020; United Nations [UN], 2021). Previous cross-national studies have assessed the impact of the percentage of people using the internet on e-participation and found a statistically significant positive impact (Åström et al., 2012; Jho & Song, 2015). Saglie and Vabo (2009) find that internet access promotes participation among youth. A UN survey (UN, 2020) shows that countries that have stronger ICT infrastructure (e.g., United States (US), United Kingdom (UK), and Republic of Korea) mostly have better e-participation as compared to countries with comparatively poorer infrastructure (e.g., India, Sri Lanka, and Uganda). Gulati et al. (2014) also argue that countries that invest more in ICT have better developed e-government and e-participation, but their data are unable to establish any relationship between ICT investment and e-participation (Gulati et al., 2014).

Chapter 3 discussed the lack or minimal consideration of the digital divide when developing the analytical framework for factors impacting e-participation in the cross-national studies. Digital divide refers to the gap in access to ICT between demographics and regions. Lack of access to the internet is found to account for lower levels of online political activity, although some argue that it does so only partially (Smith et al., 2009). However, no online interaction is possible in complete absence of ICT infrastructure. Apart from web portals, several countries have designed mobile websites and services are provided over mobile devices due to the increasing spread of mobile usage. Further, a broadband connection is shown to increase the probability of engaging in various online activities (e.g., Grubesic & Murray, 2002). Leigh and Atkinson (2001) argued that, in the future, the differences in access (or the digital divide) may not be about having internet access or not, but about having "high-speed" internet access or not (p. 16). Faster connection enables quick downloads that facilitates research and information gathering and ensures better sound and video transmission (Best & Krueger, 2005). Krueger (2002) argued that a broadband connection may enhance the likelihood of engaging in political participation. The current study argues that the availability of the ICT infrastructure improves citizen's online political engagement.

H1a: The availability of ICT infrastructure has a positive influence on e-participation.

ICT Affordability

Another determinant of e-participation resources is the cost or price of internet and mobile services in a country. Leigh and Atkinson (2001) find that broadband use is more prevalent among richer households. Increased competition in the telecommunications sector can reduce tariffs or usage costs, thus improving affordability. The affordability of ICT resources determines access by a broader group of people and whether citizens can use it for participation; thus, it influences the citizens' capacity to participate. Competition in the telecommunications sector has been used as a predictor for e-government; Gulati et al. (2014) argue that competition in the ICT industry lowers the cost of ICT and its prices to consumers and find that countries that have a more competitive telecommunications sector have more extensive development of e-government than those countries that have state-owned telecom. Further, such countries also have greater opportunities for citizen participation (Gulati et al., 2014). The current study hypothesizes that the more affordable the ICT resources, more people will have the access to, and will be able to use, ICT resources, thus influencing e-participation positively.

H1b: The affordability of ICT resources has a positive influence on e-participation.

ICT Skills

Mettler (2002) found that the educational provisions of a bill for veterans promoted their civic and political engagement and contended that policy feedback theory provided the best explanation for her findings. She argued that resource and interpretive effects of policy feedback were evident in her study as the policy increased education that affected the veterans' capacity to be involved (resource effects); this in turn made veterans notice the improvement in their well-being and life opportunities that increased their predisposition toward participation (interpretive effects). Similarly, in the e-participation literature, there is a general consensus among scholars that online skills positively influence online public participation (Anduiza et al., 2010; Best & Krueger, 2005; Krueger, 2002). Yet, an Organization for Economic Co-operation and Development (OECD, 2015) survey reported that one-fifth of adults in OECD member countries cannot work with ICT. ICT training is found to significantly improve digital literacy and the self-efficacy to use ICT applications and lessen the digital divide (Chohan & Hu, 2020). Internet skills are considered a measure of internet resources (e.g., Anduiza et al., 2010). Some scholars have found that internet skills are more important for online participation than the traditional resources of time, civic skills, or income (e.g., Anduiza et al., 2010). Actors' use of ICT for online democracy is enabled and restrained by their ICT knowledge and skills (Parvez, 2008). Consistent with past literature, the current study hypothesizes that:

H1c: ICT skills have a positive influence on e-participation.

ICT Usage – Technology in Practice

Orlikowski's (2000) technology-in-practice (or enacted technology) theory is based on Giddens' (1984) theory of structuration. The structurational model informs how sociopolitical processes shape technology, resulting in structures embedded in technology (Orlikowski, 2000). Orlikowski (2000) argues that it is only using this technology in a recurrent manner that a change can be brought about in the structure that in turn shapes the technology. Institutional arrangements including organizational characteristics influence the enactment of technology (Fountain, 2001) that shape the institutional structures, and at the same time, the recurrent usage of technology shapes the technology in use (Orlikowski, 2000).

Orlikowski's (2000) technology-in-practice lens has generated a body of research bearing the acronym PBS (practice-based studies) in the organizational and managerial research literature (Gherardi, 2009). Orlikowski (2000) applied the practice lens in an organization to study the use of Lotus Notes software in two groups in the company – one group that used the technology recurrently, and another group that was skeptical of the technology. The group using technology recurrently had a team-oriented department culture and were able to use several of its properties as well as modify the properties that served to amplify the group's view that using Lotus Notes facilitated their work and reinforced their cooperative and team-oriented department structure (Orlikowski, 2000). Tying Orlikowski's (2000) findings to the policy feedback theory, the enactment of technology displays interpretive effects both in terms of interpretation of ICT and the institutional structure around it. Mere availability of ICT does not mean that the actors will use it; instead, they will conceptualize it in different ways based on the context in which they are embedded (Orlikowski, 2000; Parvez, 2008).

Several e-gov articles cite Orlikowski's (1992; 2000) work, either as structuration theory or as a technology-in-practice lens, in overviews, discourses, and debates about e-gov (e.g., Meijer et al., 2009, 2012), in empirical research (e.g., Jiang & Xu, 2009; Parvez, 2006), and to develop propositions (Scholl, 2005). Scholl (2005) uses Orlikowski's (1992) practice lens to propose that first-order changes through electronic government reinforce e-government diffusion. As per Scholl (2005), a series of small incremental first-order changes accumulate over time to result in

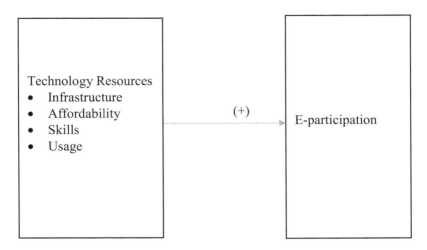

Figure 4.1 Effect of technology resources on e-participation.

a second-order change that are radical and paradigmatic. Most models of e-gov consider e-participation as a higher or advanced level application of the e-government infrastructure (e.g., Moon, 2002; Nabatchi & Mergel, 2010). Thus, usage of ICT infrastructure by individuals, government, and businesses may further promote its usage for e-participation. Following Orlikowski's (2000) technology-in-practice lens, this paper argues that mere availability of the technology is not enough to promote e-participation. Instead, the available technology needs to be used recurrently in order to affect e-participation. The more people use ICT, the more they will develop the skills and comfort in using them and the more they will find new usage for the technology (Orlikowski, 2000), such as for their engagements with government, thus influencing e-participation positively. The study hypothesizes:

H1d: Technology usage (enactment of technology) has a positive influence on e-participation.

Figure 4.1 depicts the hypothesized influence of technology resources on e-participation.

Institutional Resources

Although ICT resources are essential for e-participation, technology by itself cannot foster public participation (Åström et al., 2012; Davis, 1999; Putnam, 2000). Political institutions, such as forms of democracy

(Norris, 2011) and bureaucracies (Fountain, 2001), influence public participation. Institutional resources include laws and policies that enable the development and implementation of electronic governance (Chen & Hsieh, 2009). Such laws and policies enable agencies to work together and support the strategic direction of e-governance (Fountain, 2001). Fountain (2001) considers habits, culture, social, and professional networks also as institutional influences that influence enactment of technology. The importance of mandates is highlighted in offline public participation as well (e.g., Moynihan, 2003).

E-government began as a nonpartisan and technology-based reform, dominated by experts, and expected to attain efficiency in the public sector (West, 2005). However, governments are increasingly facing budget deficits and IT spending needs to be balanced with other expenses such as health, welfare, and defense (West, 2005). Further, rising internet usage leads to a growing number of recipients that, in turn, increases partisanship and more press coverage of digital government (West, 2005). Therefore, not only is the top management support and strong backing of politicians required but also other contextual factors such as public sector characteristics, regulations and policies for democratic participation, strong integration and active promotion of e-participation in processes and among users, and institutional and legal environment impact the implementation and outcome of e-participation initiatives (Toots, 2019). Political institutions set up the rules that can accelerate or slow down sociopolitical changes and institutions and impact political participation (Jackman & Miller, 1995; Jho & Song, 2015). The current study uses two separate measures of institutional variables: political and regulatory environment and political rights and civil liberties.

The UN e-participation index results suggest that e-participation can be promoted in different political contexts. For example, the 2014 survey results place the United States and India in the top 50 performers (of the 193 UN member countries) in e-participation. This is noteworthy because the United States has a presidential system and is a developed and high-income country, while India has a parliamentary system and is a developing and lower middle-income country. Studies argue that e-participation requires changes at the individual as well as institutional levels (West, 2005). Contextual factors of government structures are important determinants of e-participation (Gulati et al., 2014; Jho & Song, 2015; Toots, 2019; Vicente & Novo, 2014; Zheng et al., 2014). We argue that the political and regulatory environment in a country, including the efficiency and effectiveness of legislation, judicial independence, and laws relating to ICTs promote online public participation.

H2a: Supporting political environment and quality regulations for technology integration in a country has a positive influence on the e-participation in that country.

A major criticism in the public participation literature is related to the representativeness of participants: "who participates?" (Verba et al., 1993, p. 303). Studies using the resources approach stress that where power is not concentrated on a single individual there are more channels to influence policy that in turn reduces the costs of participation (e.g., Kriesi et al., 1995). Democratic institutions support citizen participation (Schlozman et al., 1999). However, Gulati et al. (2014) do not find a statistically significant relationship between a country's democracy scores and e-participation scores indicating that a more democratic political structure has no effect on the extent of a country's participatory e-government. They measure democracy by a composite index that includes Freedom House scores. Conversely, Jho and Song (2015) find that the level of democracy (as measured by the Economist Intelligence Unit [EIU] index) has a positive relationship with e-participation. They (Jho & Song, 2015), however, do not find a significant relationship between freedom of speech and e-participation.

Better political rights and civil liberties translate into empowerment of residents, especially the marginalized, which in turn can translate into more participation as well as better representativeness of participants. The current study argues that political rights and civil liberties have an interpretive effect on subsequent e-participation efforts. Political rights, such as the right to vote and to compete for public office, and civil liberties of freedom of expression and association (measures used by Freedom House) have interpretive effects of how citizens perceive their role with respect to the government and each other that can foster their participation in policymaking. These rights also engender social networks (Mettler & Sorrelle, 2018) that affect citizen's involvement in politics. The hypothesis that follows is:

H2b: Political rights and civil liberties have a positive influence on e-participation.

Figure 4.2 depicts the hypothesized influence of institutional resources on e-participation.

Technology and Institutions Influence Each Other

Technology and institutions can seldom encourage meaningful e-participation without the presence of the other. Based on policy feedback theory, this paper argues that institutions engender technology resources and interpretive effects that influences e-participation.

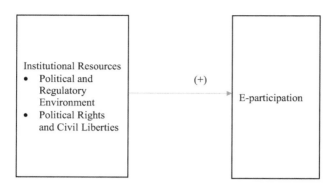

Figure 4.2 Effect of institutional resources on e-participation.

However, the socio-technical premise considers social factors and technology as intertwined in a manner that cannot be separated from each other (Sawyer & Jarrahi, 2013). Based on the theories of policy feedback and socio-technical premises, this study assesses three ways in which technology and institutions interact and influence each other that impacts e-participation: (1) institutions influence e-participation through IT resources (mediating effect of technology); (2) technology impacts e-participation by influencing policies and regulations (mediating effect of institutions); and (3) technology and institutions moderate (strengthen) the impact of each other on e-participation.

In the current study, two institutional resources – political and regulatory environment and political rights and civil liberties – are considered to facilitate or constrain ICT resources for e-participation. In the use of ICT for democratic purposes, a lot of influence is exerted by the policymakers in the design and deployment of ICT tools (Parvez, 2008) indicating the influence of institutions on the availability of technology and its use for e-participation. Parvez (2008) suggests that several factors constrain and facilitate the actors' use of ICT for e-democracy including the wider policies, institutional rules, and democratic activities and discourses surrounding e-democracy. West (2005) argues that organizational settings and political dynamics constrain the rate of technological change. A government may invite private competition in the telecom sector or keep it under its own control and such a government decision impacts the cost of the ICT infrastructure. This has a policy feedback effect on e-participation as it determines the affordability of ICT resources for the citizens to participate. Institutions also influence citizen's trust, efficacy, satisfaction, and political attitude, thus influencing citizen participation (Marien & Christensen, 2013; Norris et al., 2006; Vicente & Novo, 2014).

There is scarce work in the area of the link between development of online public administration and citizen e-participation (Vicente & Novo, 2014). One study shows weak association between the efforts made by local authorities to stimulate e-participation and citizens' online engagement (Saglie & Vabo, 2009; as cited in Vicente & Novo, 2014). The government actors in another study expressed the view that the ICT use policies hindered their use of ICT (Parvez, 2008). Countries with better administration and governance and policies supporting ICT such as competition in the telecommunications sector have better provisions of e-participation such as more online services presence (Gulati et al., 2014). Public policies affect people's civic engagement or involvement in politics (Mettler & Sorrelle, 2018), for example, educational policies engender public participation through endowment of skills, resources, and social networks (Verba et al., 1995).

Political rights and civil liberties such as the rule of law, a free and independent media, academic freedom, the freedom to establish private business, free trade unions, interest groups, professional and private organizations, the absence of economic exploitation, and protection from political terror (Freedom House, 2012) have resource and interpretive effects that influence citizen perceptions to use ICT resources for e-participation. For example, Freedom House (2015) reports that more and more governments are pressurizing private companies to implement censorship on the internet content and dissidents face blockage and loss of business. The companies providing ICT infrastructure are thus vulnerable to the local laws and authorities, which impacts the technology resources of ICT availability, affordability, and skill development negatively. Further, such censorships discourage residents from using available ICT resources for participatory activities through interpretive effects as citizens may consider usage of ICT infrastructure for participation detrimental to their well-being or something that is perceived as anti-government. In other cases, governments curb ICT usage for political activities by coercing individuals to remove content, harassing, and prosecuting those who refuse to follow the diktat (Freedom House, 2015). Thus, in such countries where political rights and civil liberties are limited, institutions are hindering the provision and usage of technology resources for e-participation. Therefore, this study hypothesizes that,

H3a: Technology acts as a mediator for the institutions' impact on e-participation.

However, actor–network theory (Callon & Law 1989; Latour, 1987), under the socio-technical premises, considers technology as an actor in its own right that has an ability to bend the intentions and will of the political actors around it, for example, the development of cheaper and efficient ICT solutions may lead governments to promote policies for its deployment to attain their goals of global competitiveness or sustainability. Technology enactment induces a feedback effect of learning. The structuration theory scholars suggest that human actors are not passive receivers of ICT as they can comply with the rules for ICT use or modify (or change) it through ICT usage, leading to intended and unintended consequences even in social structures (Orlikowski, 2000; Parvez, 2008). Social structures are the rules and actions that enable or constrain the actors and are both a medium and product of human action; the human action in this case is the usage of ICT for online participation (Giddens, 1984; Parvez, 2008). Thus, ICT resources in the current study also have the potential to influence the institutional resources so that they are further developed to promote or constrain e-participation. To develop a theoretical model of e-participation that accounts for the likely reciprocity between technology and institutional variables (Best & Krueger, 2005), the current study hypothesizes that:

H3b: Institutions act as a mediator for technology's impact on e-participation.

E-participation requires the necessary technological infrastructure and access and know-how of ICT tools and their usage by both the public and government. At the same time, organizational settings, cultural, and political dynamics constrain the transformative potential of technology change like e-participation (West, 2005). Institutions, by virtue of their regulation power, affect e-participation (Jho & Song, 2015). Laudon (1977) considered technology only as a facilitating factor, interacting with the organizational and environmental forces to shape the future. Jho and Song (2015) examine the effect of interaction between technology and institutions on e-participation. They find a positive relationship between technology (online population) and e-participation but do not find a significant relationship between political institution and e-participation, when each factor is evaluated independently (Jho & Song, 2015). However, for the moderating effects between technology and institutions, they find that high levels of e-participation are associated with the interaction of technological infrastructure and the political institutions such as freedom of speech and association and the level of democracy (Jho & Song, 2015). Jho and Song's study evaluates the moderating effects of institutions on technology by using a single measure of technology (percentage of individuals using the internet). The current study uses multiple dimensions of technology (ICT infrastructure, affordability, skills, and usage) and institutions

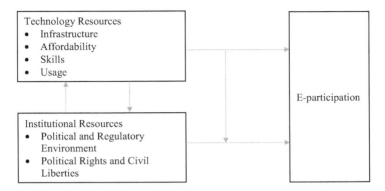

Figure 4.3 Moderation and mediation effects of technology and institutions on e-participation.

(political and regulatory environment and political rights and civil liberties) and assesses their interaction effect on e-participation. The current study hypothesizes that:

H4: Technology and institutions interact to influence e-participation.

Exploring both technological and institutional resources as moderating and mediating variables informs the path and the intertwined complex nature of the relation between these resources and e-participation. These hypothesized effects of moderation and mediation are depicted in Figure 4.3.

Influence of Factors at Different Levels of E-Participation

The current study explores the impact of technology and institutional factors on the degree, as well as the levels, of e-participation. In the UN's survey, e-participation is measured using the scores of its three stages of e-information, e-consultation, and e-decision making (UN, 2014). Each member country gets a percentage score based on utilization of e-participation at each of the three levels of participation as well as a cumulative e-participation score. There is a significant difference in the utilization of e-participation in the three stages, even among the top 50 performers. For example, both the United States and India are in the top 50 performers based on the overall e-participation score in 2014, but their percentage utilization across different stages of e-participation varies significantly; while both countries' scores for the e-information stage are above 90 percent, India failed to score even a single point in e-decision making, while the United States scored 89 percent. The literature review and subsequent gap analysis indicates that studies to date have largely ignored differences in factors for the utilization of e-participation by separate levels (or stages). Some recent studies have incorporated different levels of participation in their models (Khan & Krishnan, 2020; Krishnan et al., 2017). Khan and Krishnan (2020) find a positive influence of virtual social networks diffusion in a country on the implementation of the three stages of e-participation via national governance and IT governance mechanisms. Anduiza et al. (2010) studied three different types of online participation in Spain: contacting representatives, donating money, and raising petitions. Their study finds differences in the resources and their magnitude across different types of online participation activities.

The types of activities advance in complexity as one moves to higher stages of e-participation. As compared to the initial stages of information sharing, the later stages of e-participation require higher levels of interoperability and more sophisticated technology solutions for encryption, information sharing, and interactive communication (Hiller & Belanger, 2001; Moon, 2002). The e-information stage is associated with static and one-way communication; e-information stage requires ICT infrastructure and skills to upload, download, send, receive, and interpret information. The e-consultation stage involves dynamic two-way communication; this stage additionally requires access to social networking sites and better online skills to communicate on these sites for the purpose of providing feedback on government policies and decision making. Internet bandwidth and institutional regulations also become important at this stage for enabling the two-way communication. The e-decision-making stage is associated with empowerment of residents. The institutional resources, including greater levels of political rights and civil liberties, are required for the higher stages of e-participation as the power sharing between government and citizens changes with more delegation and control provided to citizens. We argue that the resources required and their impact are not similar across the three levels of e-participation – e-information, e-consultation, and e-decision making. More sophisticated levels of e-participation will require strengthened technological and institutional resources. The second research question that this study explores is: Do the factors differ in their influence on e-information, e-consultation, and e-decision-making levels? The difference in the magnitude and significance of technology and institutional factors influencing e-participation utilization for the three different stages is evaluated in this study. The hypothesis is that:

Table 4.1 A list of all hypotheses

Direct impact of technology	H1a: The availability of ICT infrastructure has a positive influence on e-participation. H1b: The affordability of ICT resources has a positive influence on e-participation. H1c: ICT skills have a positive influence on e-participation. H1d: Technology usage (enactment of technology) has a positive influence on e-participation.
Direct impact of institutions	H2a: Supporting political and regulatory environment in a country has a positive influence on the e-participation in that country. H2b: Political rights and civil liberties have a positive influence on e-participation.
Mediation Analysis	H3a: Technology acts as a mediator for the institutions' impact on e-participation. H3b: Institutions act as a mediator for technology's impact on e-participation
Interaction of institutions and technology	H4: Technology and institutions interact to influence e-participation.
Factors at different levels of e-participation	H5: There is a difference in the technology and institutional resources for different levels of e-participation.

H5: There is a difference in the technology and institutional resources for different levels of e-participation.

Table 4.1 provides a comprehensive list of all hypotheses analyzed in the current study.

Data – Measures and Sources

The variables of technology and institutions are operationalized using secondary data. The data used in this study are from international organizations of repute, are used in previous studies across different fields, and are updated as they are assessed on a yearly or biennial basis.

The Dependent Variable: E-Participation

The dependent variables for the current study are e-participation and its levels of e-information, e-consultation, and e-decision making. To measure these variables, the study uses the e-participation scores of countries in the UN survey for the years 2012, 2014, 2016, and 2018. The UN e-participation survey assesses how countries are using online services to promote citizen-to-citizen and citizen-to-government interaction and availability and relevance of participatory services in a country. The UN (2014) e-participation framework defines e-information as "enabling participation by providing citizens with public information and access to information without or upon demand," e-consultation as "engaging citizens in contributions to and deliberation on public policies and services," and e-decision making as "empowering citizens through co-design of policy options and co-production of service components and delivery modalities" (p. 197).

Prior cross-national studies have used the scores of UN surveys to measure e-participation (e.g., Åström et al., 2012; Gulati et al., 2014; Jho & Song, 2015; Zhao et al., 2014). This study is additionally using the percentage scores of e-participation utilizations by the three levels. The e-information stage assesses websites for availability of archived information on policies and acts, budgets, and online information on citizens' right to government information, across the six sectors of finance, health, labor, education, social welfare, and environment for assessment of the e-information stage (UN, 2014). E-consultation is assessed through evidence of use of website features and tools for e-consultation such as social media, online discussion forums, and online polls (UN, 2014). E-decision making assesses evidence of consultation inputs incorporated in government decisions in the six sectors and sharing of outcomes of online participation (UN, 2014).

The UN updated the parameters for assessing e-participation and its utilization by different stages over the years, yet the definitions remain the same and the scores capture performance of the countries relative to one another for a given year. E-participation surveys from the UN assess how countries are using ICT tools for encouraging online interaction between government and citizens through provision of information, interaction with stakeholders, and engaging citizens in decision-making processes. Studies in the past (e.g., Åström et al., 2012) have successfully combined and analyzed UN survey data in longitudinal studies.

Explanatory Variables

In the current study, the explanatory variables are divided into the two categories of technology resources and institutional resources. The technology variables are measured using data from the Network Readiness Index (NRI) of the World Economic Forum (WEF). The NRI index measures the ICT status of countries, and the current study employs its scores for the dimensions of infrastructure, affordability, skills, and usage of ICTs (WEF, 2016). The indicators are measured using data obtained through surveys and data from other international agencies such as the UN and the World Bank. The current study uses the scores for the years 2012, 2014, and 2016 for the indicators of infrastructure, affordability, skills, and individual, business, and government usage. The infrastructure component measures electricity production, mobile coverage, internet bandwidth, and internet servers available for the population (WEF, 2016). The affordability indicator measures tariffs and competition index for cellular and fixed broadband internet and mobile communication (WEF, 2016). Skills measure gross enrollment in secondary education, adult literacy, and quality of math and science education in a country (WEF, 2016). The ICT usage data are measured across three dimensions: Individual usage data measures the percentage of individuals or households with computers, mobile devices, internet access, broadband subscriptions, or that use social virtual networks; business usage measures technology absorption and innovation capacity at the firm level, and use of ICT in business-to-business and business-to-customer engagements; government usage data measures the importance of ICTs in government's vision, government's online service index (a component of UN's e-government survey), and government's success in promoting ICT (WEF, 2016). Separately assessing the impacts of the four technology dimensions, instead of composite NRI score, provides better actionable feedback to practitioners and helps filter items that are not of interest.

The data for the institutional variable of political and regulatory environment are also obtained from WEF's NRI study. Some e-participation studies in the past evaluate laws and policies such as implementation of online privacy and security laws (e.g., Chen & Hsieh, 2009). Apart from privacy and security laws, regulatory quality has been used by Gulati et al. (2014) in an e-participation model as a governance indicator. The current study utilizes the scores of political and regulatory environments in the WEF survey. This index is comprised of an assessment of laws relating to ICTs in a country, effectiveness of law-making bodies, intellectual property protection, and software piracy rate in a country among other indicators (WEF, 2016).

The scores for the institutional variable of political rights and civil liberties are obtained from the Freedom House index. Freedom House is a US-based nongovernmental organization, established in 1941, and its data are widely used in previous studies for measuring the institutionalization of freedom of speech and association or democratic politics in a country (such as by Gulati et al., 2014; Jho & Song, 2015). Freedom House assesses the rights and freedoms enjoyed by individuals in the real world, for example, political participation, pluralism, electoral processes, personal autonomy, rights to associate and organize, freedom of belief and expression, and functioning of government (Freedom House, 2016).

Political rights and civil liberties data were reverse coded because, in the original dataset, low values of these measures denotes high democracy levels. This is in reverse sense of the other variables such as e-participation where low values denote low e-participation. The mean value of political rights and civil liberties is used to represent a single variable of "political rights and civil liberties" in the model. The two terms are highly correlated with a correlation of $r > 0.9$. A single value for these two variables is available in the original dataset from Freedom House but only for the year 2016. Since the current study is using 2012, 2014, and 2016 data, the value was calculated by taking a mean of the two scores.

Control Variables

This study uses the socioeconomic and demographic variables as the control variables; these consist of national income (measured by gross domestic product [GDP] per capita), percentage of young in the population, and urban population percentage. Gulati et al. (2014) use percentage of residents living in urban areas as a measure for urbanization and so does the current study; Zhao et al. (2014) use the World Bank's gross national income per capita to measure economic development in a country to differentiate the impact on e-government between high- and low-income countries. This study uses GDP per capita because of the availability of these data for a larger number of countries in the three years of survey data used. All variables, measures, and data sources used in the current study are aggregated in the Appendix. The full conceptual model of e-participation along with the control variables is depicted in Figure 4.4. The model, as shown in Figure 4.4, is the Policy Feedback and Socio-Technological Approach to E-participation (see Rawat, 2020). The model argues that it is the complex relationship between various dimensions of technology and institutional resources that influence e-participation and its various stages.

Sample

The unit of analysis in the current study is a country. The population for the current study comprises of all countries in the world. The sampling frame is the list of countries that are UN members and for which the data for the dependent variable of e-participation are available in the

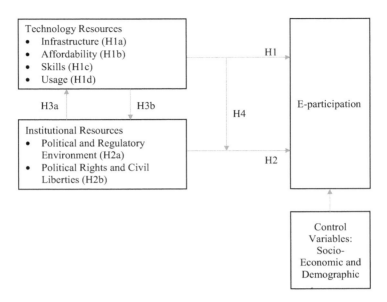

Figure 4.4 Model for the analysis of impact of institutions and technology on e-participation (adapted from Rawat, 2020).

UN survey. This provides the base list of countries for the study. Due to the nonavailability of the data for the explanatory variables, some countries are removed from the final dataset. The current study uses panel data for 143 countries. The data were first downloaded, copied, and arranged in a single excel sheet and then imported in Stata tool for analysis. All the dependent and explanatory variables are continuous variables.

References

Anduiza, E., Gallego, A., & Cantijoch, M. (2010). Online political participation in Spain: The impact of traditional and internet resources. *Journal of Information Technology & Politics, 7*(4), 356–368.

Åström, J., Karlsson, M., Linde, J., & Pirannejad, A. (2012). Understanding the rise of e-participation in non-democracies: Domestic and international factors. *Government Information Quarterly, 29*(2), 142–150.

Avgerou, C. (2001). The significance of context in information systems and organizational change. *Information Systems Journal, 11*(1), 43–63.

Best, S., & Krueger, J. (2005). Analyzing the representativeness of internet political participation. *Political Behavior, 27*(2), 183–216.

Bostrom, R. P., & Heinen, J. S. (1977a). MIS problems and failures: A socio-technical perspective. Part I: The causes. *MIS Quarterly, 1*, 17–32.

Bostrom, R. P., & Heinen, J. S. (1977b). MIS problems and failures: A socio-technical perspective, Part II: The application of socio-technical theory. *MIS Quarterly, 1*, 11–28.

Bwalya, K. J., Plessis, T. D., & Rensleigh, C. (2014). E-government implementation in Zambia – Prospects. *Transforming Government: People, Process and Policy, 8*(1), 101–130.

Callon, M., and J. Law. (1989). On the construction of sociotechnical networks: Content and context revisited. *Knowledge and Society, 8*, 57–83.

Campbell, A. L. (2003). *How policies make citizens: Senior political activism and the American welfare state*. Princeton, NJ: Princeton University Press.

Campbell, A. L. (2012). Policy makes mass politics. *Annual Review of Political Science, 15*, 333–351.

Chai, S., & Kim, M. (2012). A socio-technical approach to knowledge contribution behavior: An empirical investigation of social networking sites users. *International Journal of Information Management, 32*(2), 118–126.

Chen, Y., & Hsieh, J. (2009). Advancing e-governance: Comparing Taiwan and the United States. *Public Administration Review, 69*(S1), S151–S158. doi:10.1111/j.1540-6210.2009.02103.x.

Chohan, S. R., & Hu, G. (2020). Strengthening digital inclusion through e-government: Cohesive ICT training programs to intensify digital competency. *Information Technology for Development*. Open access. https://doi.org/10.1080/02681102.2020.1841713.

Davis, R. (1999). *The web of politics: The internet's impact on the American political system*. New York, NY: Oxford University Press.

Eisinger, P. (1973). The conditions of protest behavior in American cities. *The American Political Science Review, 67*(1), 11–28.

Fountain, J. (2001). *Building the virtual state information technology and institutional change*. Washington, DC: Brookings Institution Press.

Fountain, J. (2006). Enacting technology in networked governance: Developmental processes of cross-agency arrangements. National Center for Digital Government, Paper 16. Retrieved from http://scholarworks.umass.edu/ncdg/16. Accessed on May 12, 2021.

Freedom House. (2012). Freedom in the world 2012. Retrieved from https://freedomhouse.org/report/freedom-world/freedom-world-2012. Accessed on June 3, 2021.

Freedom House. (2015). Freedom in the world 2015. Retrieved from https://freedomhouse.org/report/freedom-world/freedom-world-2015#.WwQ5Jy_Mw0o. Accessed on June 3, 2021.

Freedom House. (2016). Freedom in the World 2016 Methodology. Retrieved from https://freedomhouse.org/sites/default/files/2020-02/Methodology_FIW_2016.pdf. Accessed on March 14, 2021.

Geels, F. (2004). From sectoral systems of innovation to socio-technical systems: Insights about dynamics and change from sociology and institutional theory. *Research Policy, 33*(6), 897–920.

Gherardi, S. (2009). Introduction: The critical power of the 'practice lens'. *Management Learning, 40*(2), 115–128.

Giddens, A. (1984). *The constitution of society: Outline of the theory of structuration.* Cambridge: Polity Press.

Gil-Garcia, J. (2012). *Enacting electronic government success* (Vol. 31, Integrated Series in Information Systems). Boston, MA: Springer US.

Gil-Garcia, R., & Pardo, T. A. (2006). Multi-method approaches to understanding the complexity of e-government. *International Journal of Computers, Systems and Signals, 7*(2), 3–17.

Grubesic, T., & Murray, A. (2002). Constructing the divide: Spatial disparities in broadband access. *Papers in Regional Science, 81*, 197–221.

Gulati, G., Williams, C. B., & Yates, D. J. (2014). Predictors of on-line services and e-participation: A cross-national comparison. *Government Information Quarterly, 3*(1), 526–533. doi:10.1016/j.giq.2014.07.005.

Hacker, J. S., & Pierson, P. (2014). After the master theory: Downs, Schattschneider, and the rebirth of policy-focused analysis. *Perspectives on Politics, 12*(3), 643–662.

Hansen, H. S., & Reinau, K. H. (2006). The citizens in e-participation. In M. A. Wimmer, H. J. Scholl, Å. Grönlund, & K. V. Andersen (Eds.) *Electronic government* (pp. 70–82). 5th International Conference, EGOV 2006, Kraków, Poland, September 4–8, 2006 Proceedings. Berlin: Springer.

Hiller, J., & Belanger, F. (2001). Privacy strategies for electronic government. E-Government Series. Arlington, VA: PricewaterhouseCoopers Endowment for the Business of Government. Retrieved from www.businessofgovernment. org/sites/default/files/PrivacyStrategies.pdf. Accessed on June 3, 2021.

International Telecommunication Union (ITU). (2020). Measuring digital development: Facts and figures, 2020. Retrieved from www.itu.int/en/ITU-D/Statistics/Documents/facts/FactsFigures2020.pdf. Accessed on February 16, 2021.

Jackman, R. W., & Miller, R. A. (1995). Voter turnout in the industrial democracies during the 1980s. *Comparative Political Studies, 27*, 467–492.

Jho, W., & Song, K. J. (2015). Institutional and technological determinants of civil e-participation: Solo or duet? *Government Information Quarterly, 3*(2), 488–495. doi:10.1016/j.giq.2015.09.003.

Jiang, M., & Xu, H. (2009). Exploring online structures on Chinese government portals. *Social Science Computer Review, 27*(2), 174–195.

Khan, A., & Krishnan, S. (2020). Virtual social networks diffusion, governance mechanisms, and e-participation implementation: A cross-country investigation. *E-Service Journal, 11*(3), 36–69. doi:10.2979/eservicej.11.3.02.

Kling, R. (1980). Social analyses of computing: Theoretical perspectives in recent empirical research. *ACM Computing Surveys (CSUR), 12*(1), 61–110.

Kling, R., & Lamb, R. (2000). IT and organizational change in digital economies: A sociotechnical approach. In E. Brynjolfsson & B. Kahin (Eds.), *Understanding the digital economy. Data, tools, and research.* Cambridge, MA: The MIT Press.

Kling, R., McKim, G., & King, A. (2003). A bit more to it: Scholarly communication forums as socio-technical interaction networks. *Journal of the American Society for Information Science and Technology, 54*(1), 47–67.

Kriesi, H., Koopmans, R., & Duyvendak, J. (1995). *New social movements in Western Europe: A comparative analysis.* London: UCL Press.

Krishna, A. (Ed.). (2008). *Poverty, participation and democracy: A global perspective.* New York, NY: Cambridge University Press.

Krishnan, S., Teo, T. S., & Lymm, J. (2017). Determinants of electronic participation and electronic government maturity: Insights from cross-country data. *International Journal of Information Management, 37*(4), 297–312.

Krueger, B. S. (2002). Assessing the potential of internet political participation in the United States: A resource approach. *American Politics Research, 30*(5), 476–498.

Latour, B. (1987). *Science in action: How to follow scientists and engineers through society.* Cambridge, MA: Harvard University Press.

Laudon, K. (1977). *Communications technology and democratic participation* (Praeger special studies in US economic, social, and political issues). New York, NY: Praeger.

Lazarsfled, P., Berelson, B., & Gaudet, H. (1948). *The people's choice: How the voter makes up his mind in a presidential campaign.* New York, NY: Columbia University Press.

Leigh, A., & Atkinson, R. (2001). *Clear thinking on the digital divide.* Washington, DC: Progressive Policy Institute.

Lowi, T. J. (1972). Four systems of policy, politics, and choice. *Public Administration Review, 32*(4), 298–310. doi:10.2307/974990.

Marien, S., & Christensen, H. (2013). Trust and openness: Prerequisites for democratic engagement. In K. N. Demetriou (Ed.), *Democracy in transition. Political participation in the European Union* (pp. 109–134). New York, NY: Springer.

McCarthy, J. D., & Zald, M. N. (2001). The enduring vitality of the resource mobilization theory of social movements. In J. Turner (Ed.), *Handbook of sociological theory* (pp. 533–567). Berlin: Springer eBooks.

Meijer, A., Burger, N., & Ebbers, W. (2009). Citizens 4 citizens: Mapping participatory practices on the internet. *Electronic Journal of E-Government, 7*(1), 99–112.

Meijer, A., Koops, B., Pieterson, W., Overman, S., & Ten Tije, S. (2012). Government 2.0: Key challenges to its realization. *Electronic Journal of E-Government, 10*(1), 59–69.

Mettler, S. (2002). Bringing the state back in to civic engagement: Policy feedback effects of the G.I. Bill for World War II veterans. *American Political Science Review, 96*(2), 351–365.

Mettler, S. & Sorrelle, M. (2018). Policy feedback theory. In C.M. Weible & P.A. Sabatier (Eds.), *Theories of the policy process* – 4th edition, pp. 103–134. Boulder, CO: Westview Press.

Mettler, S., & Soss, J. (2004). The consequences of public policy for democratic citizenship: Bridging policy studies and mass politics. *Perspectives on Politics, 2*(1), 55–73.

Mettler, S., & Welch, E. (2004). Civic generation: Policy feedback effects of the GI Bill on political involvement over the life course. *British Journal of Political Science, 34*, 497–518.

Moon, M. (2002). The evolution of e-government among municipalities: Rhetoric or reality? *Public Administration Review, 62*(4), 424–433.

Moynihan, D. P. (2003). Normative and instrumental perspectives on public participation: Citizen summits in Washington, DC. *American Review of Public Administration, 33*(2), 164–188.

Moynihan, D. P., & Soss, J. (2014). Policy feedback and the politics of administration. *Public Administration Review, 74*(3), 320–332. https://doi.org/10.1111/puar.12200.

Nabatchi, T., & Mergel, I. (2010). Participation 2.0: Using Internet and social media technologies to promote distributed democracy and create digital neighborhoods. In J. H. Svara & J. Denhardt (Eds.), *Connected communities: Local governments as a partner in citizen engagement and community building* (pp. 80–87). Phoenix, AZ: Alliance for Innovation.

Norris, P. (2001). *Digital divide: Civic engagement, information poverty, and the internet worldwide*. Cambridge: Cambridge University Press.

Norris, P. (2011). *Democratic deficit*. Cambridge: Cambridge University Press.

Norris, P., Walgrave, S., & Van Aelst, P. (2006). Does protest signify disaffection? Demonstrators in a postindustrial democracy. In M. Torcal, & J. R. Montero (Eds.), *Political disaffection in contemporary democracies: Social capital, institutions and politics* (pp. 279–307). New York, NY: Routledge.

Organization for Economic Co-operation and Development (OECD). (2015). OECD skills studies. Retrieved from www.oecd-ilibrary.org/education/adults-computers-and-problem-solving_9789264236844-en;jsessionid=1cm271f7ue5ej.x-oecd-live-02. Accessed on February 3, 2017.

Orlikowski, W. J. (1992). The duality of technology: Rethinking the concept of technology in organizations. *Organization Science, 3*(3), 398–427.

Orlikowski, W. J. (2000). Using technology and constituting structures: A practice lens for studying technology in organizations. *Organization Science, 4*, 404.

Orlikowski, W. J., & Iacono, C. S. (2001). Research commentary: Desperately seeking the "IT" in IT research – A call to theorizing the IT artifact. *Information Systems Research, 12*(2), 121–134.

Parvez, Z. (2006). Informatization of local democracy: A structuration perspective. *Information Polity, 11*(1), 67–83.

Parvez, Z. (2008). E-democracy from the perspective of local elected members. *International Journal of Electronic Government Research (IJEGR), 4*(3), 20–35.

Patashnik, E. M. (2008). *Reforms at risk: What happens after major policy changes are enacted*. Princeton, NJ: Princeton University Press.

Pierson, P. (1993). When effect becomes cause: Policy feedback and political change. *World Politics, 45*(4), 595–628.

Pierson, P. (1994). *Dismantling the Welfare state? Reagan, Thatcher, and the politics of retrenchment*. New York, NY: Cambridge University Press.

Porwol, L., Ojo, A., & Breslin, J. (2013). On the duality of e-participation – Towards a foundation for citizen-led participation. In A. Kő, C. Leitner, H. Leitold, & A. Prosser (Eds.), *Technology-enabled innovation for democracy, government and governance*. EGOVIS/EDEM 2013. Lecture Notes in Computer Science, Vol. 8061. Berlin: Springer.

Putnam, R. (2000). *Bowling alone: The collapse and revival of American community*. New York, NY: Simon & Schuster.

Rawat, P. (2020). A policy feedback and socio-technical approach to e-participation (PFSTEP): A cross-national analysis of technology and institutions to explain e-participation. *Journal of Information Technology & Politics*, 1–16. doi:10.1080/19331681.2020.1839621.

Saglie, J., & Vabo, S. (2009). Size and e-democracy: Online participation in Norwegian local politics. *Scandinavian Political Studies*, *32*(4), 382–401.

Sawyer, S. (2006). Social informatics: Overview, principles and opportunities. *Bulletin of the American Society for Information Science and Technology*, *31*(5), 9–12.

Sawyer, S., & Jarrahi, M. (2013). The sociotechnical perspective. In A. Tucker & H. Topi (Eds.) *CRC handbook of computing*. Chapman and Hall (in press). Retrieved from http://sawyer.syr.edu/publications/2013/sociotechnical%20 chapter.pdf. Accessed on January 20, 2017.

Schattschneider, E. (1935). *Politics, pressures and the tariff: A study of free private enterprise in pressure politics, as shown in the 1929-1930 revision of the tariff* (Prentice-Hall political science series). New York, NY: Prentice-Hall.

Schlozman, K. L., Verba, S., & Brady, H. (1999). Civic participation and the equality problem. In T. Skocpol & M. Fiorina (Eds.), *Civic engagement in American democracy* (pp. 427–459). Washington, DC: Brookings Institution.

Scholl, H. J. (2005). Organizational transformation through e-government: Myth or reality? In: M. A. Wimmer, R. Traunmüller, Å. Grönlund, & K. V. Andersen (Eds.), *Electronic government*. EGOV 2005. Lecture Notes in Computer Science, Vol. 3591. Berlin: Springer.

Senyucel, Z. (2007). Assessing the impact of e-government on providers and users of the IS function: A structuration perspective. *Transforming Government: People, Process and Policy, 1*(2), 131–144.

Skocpol, T. (1992). *Protecting soldiers and mothers: The political origins of social policy in the United States*. Cambridge, MA: The Belknap Press of Harvard University Press.

Smith, A., Schlozman, K. L., Verba, S., & Brady, H. (2009). The demographics of online and offline political participation. Retrieved from www. pewinternet.org/2009/09/01/the-demographics-of-online-and-offline-politicalparticipation/. Accessed on December 14, 2020.

Soss, J., Fording, R., & Schram, S. (2011). *Disciplining the poor: Neoliberal paternalism and the persistent power of race*. Chicago, IL: University of Chicago Press.

Taylor, F. (1967). *The principles of scientific management.* New York, NY: Norton.

Toots, M. (2019). Why e-participation systems fail: The case of Estonia's Osale. ee. *Government Information Quarterly, 36*(3), 546–559. https://doi.org/ 10.1016/j.giq.2019.02.002.

Trist, E. L. (1981). The evolution of socio-technical systems. Retrieved from http://sistemas-humano-computacionais.wdfiles.com/local--files/capit ulo%3Aredes-socio-tecnicas/Evolution_of_socio_technical_systems.pdf. Accessed on April 3, 2017.

Trist, E. L. (1989). The assumptions of ordinariness as a denial mechanism: Innovation and conflict in a coal mine. *Human Resource Management (1986-1998), 28*(2), 253.

Trist, E. L., Higgin, G. W., Murray, H., & Pollock, A. B. (1963). *Organizational choice: Capabilities of groups at the coal face under changing technologies.* London: Tavistock Publications.

United Nations (UN). (2014). E-government survey 2014. Retrieved from https://publicadministration.un.org/egovkb/en-us/Reports/UN-E-Governm ent-Survey-2014. Accessed on June 3, 2021.

United Nations (UN). (2020). E-government survey 2020. Retrieved from https://publicadministration.un.org/egovkb/en-us/Reports/UN-E-Governm ent-Survey-2020. Accessed on June 3, 2021.

United Nations (UN). (2021, May 25). Digital connectivity essential for least developed countries to reap benefits of fourth industrial revolution, experts tell preparatory committee. LDC5 Preparatory Committee, First Session, Press Release DEV 3439. Retrieved from www.un.org/press/en/2021/ dev3439.doc.htm. Accessed on June 3, 2021.

Verba, S. (1996). The citizen as respondent: Sample surveys and American democracy. *American Political Science Review, 90*, 1–7.

Verba, S., Nie, N. H., & Kim, J. (1978). *Participation and political equality: A seven-nation comparison.* Cambridge: Cambridge University Press. Verba, S., Schlozman, K., & Brady, H. (1995) *Voice and equality: Civic voluntarism in American politics.* Cambridge, MA: Harvard University Press.

Verba, S., Schlozman, K., Brady, H., & Nie, N. H. (1993). Citizen activity: Who participates? What do they say? *American Political Science Review, 87*(2), 303–318.

Vicente, M. R., & Novo, A. (2014). An empirical analysis of e-participation. The role of social networks and e-government over citizens' online engagement. *Government Information Quarterly, 31*(3), 379–387.

Weerakkody, V., Dwivedi, Y. K., Brooks, L., Williams, M. D., Mwange, A. (2007). E-government implementation in Zambia: Contributing factors. *Electronic Government, an International Journal, 4* (4), 484–508.

West, D. (2005). *Digital government technology and public sector performance* (Safari tech books online ed.). Princeton, NJ: Princeton University Press.

World Economic Forum (WEF). (2016). Networked readiness index. Retrieved from www3.weforum.org/docs/GITR2016/GITR_2016_full%20report_ final.pdf. Accessed on June 3, 2021.

Zhao, F., Shen, K., & Collier, A. (2014). Effects of national culture on e-government diffusion – A global study of 55 countries. *Information & Management, 51*(8), 1005–1016.

Zheng, Y., Schachter, H. L., & Holzer, M. (2014). The impact of government form on e-participation: A study of New Jersey municipalities. *Government Information Quarterly, 3*(1), 653–659.

5 How Do Technology and Institutions Impact E-Participation?

Analyzing the Impact of Technology and Institutions

This research hypothesizes complex relationships between technology, institutions, and e-participation. The study uses the following analysis methods for testing the hypotheses.

Direct Effects and Mediation Analysis

This chapter evaluates the direct and mediating role of technology as well as institutional resources. Therefore, there are two models to be evaluated – one each for technology and institution as mediator. The cross-lagged panel model, a type of simultaneous equation modeling (SEM), is used to test the direct and indirect effects of hypotheses (H1, H2, H3). Simultaneous equations are analyzed using the structural part of the SEM for each variable used in the model and provides the direct, indirect, and total effects of technology and institution resources on e-participation. SEM is a set of equations with joint dependencies of variables wherein one or more of the explanatory variables are jointly determined with the dependent variable (Wooldridge, 2000). For example, when analyzing institutions as the mediator, e-participation and institutions are the two endogenous variables. Technology variables, in this analysis, are exogenous (or predictor variables). Cross-lagged panel model (CLPM) is a type of SEM used to assess the impact of independent variable X at time t on the dependent variable Y at time $t + 1$. CLPM is used in the current study to analyze direct and mediation effects for three years of survey data – 2012, 2014, and 2016 (see Figure 5.1). When analyzing institutions as the mediator, the CLPM assesses the impact of technology in 2012 on institutions in 2014, and the indirect effect via institutions on e-participation in year 2016.

DOI: 10.4324/9781003164326-5

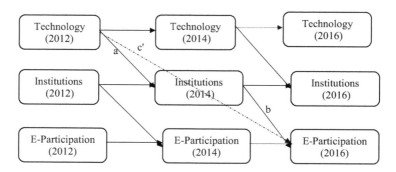

Figure 5.1 Cross-lagged panel model analyzing mediation impact of institutional resources.

Note: ab = mediation or indirect effect size; c' = leftover direct effect of technology (2012) on e-participation (2016)

Maximum likelihood estimation is used. It is the default in Stata as well as the most frequently used estimation method (Ullman, 2006).

Moderator Analysis

Following Jho and Song's (2015) data analysis for interaction effects of technology and institutions, we employ *t*-test and analysis of covariance (ANCOVA) for testing the moderator hypothesis (H4) with the 2012, 2014, and 2016 data. The countries are divided into two groups of low and high e-participation, where the former group has countries with e-participation scores below the mean score of all countries and the latter group is comprised of the countries with e-participation scores higher than the mean e-participation score of all countries. The *t*-test is conducted to assess the difference in mean of each explanatory variable for the two groups of countries. The ANCOVA provides the interaction terms for both institutional variables with each technology variable.

Factors for Levels of E-Participation

The current study also assesses the impact of the explanatory variables on distinct e-participation levels. Multivariate regression is applied for the last hypothesis (H5) of difference in the magnitude and significance of technology and institution variables across the three stages of e-information, e-consultation, and e-decision making. Multivariate regression is used to assess the technology and institutional resources for the three levels of e-information, e-consultation, and e-decision making. The multivariate analysis uses United Nations (UN) e-government survey data of 2014, 2016, and 2018 for the three dependent variables of e-information, e-consultation, and e-decision making. This is because the 2012 UN published report does not have the data for the three stages for all countries. The institutions and technology data used are for years 2012, 2014, and 2016 that create a lag of two years between the explanatory and dependent variables given the understanding that changes in institutions and technology may not have an immediate impact on e-information, e-consultation, and e-decision making. Chapter 4 discussed how e-government research is different from traditional information systems research and that the transformational impacts of e-government practice take time to become visible and to bring about a higher order change like e-participation (Scholl, 2005). This is also consistent with policy feedback theory that suggests the current policies engender resources for future participation. The list of all models in testing the hypotheses is provided in Table 5.1.

Results and Analysis

Description and Summary

The e-participation data are summarized in Table 5.2. The number of observations is 143 for each of the three years, the total number of country/year observations. The range for dependent variable e-participation in 2014 is from 0.0196 to 1 with a mean of 0.47. The minimum value in the range for the first stage, e-information, in 2014 is 7.41, while that for e-consultation and e-decision making is 0. A minimum non-zero value of 7.41 means that all 143 countries have at least some level of e-information (i.e., online sharing of desired information on policies and government actions on national government websites) for one or more of the six departments analyzed in the UN e-participation surveys. A maximum value of 100 on e-information indicates that one or more countries have all (100 percent) policy documents and desired government information shared online. The minimum value of 0 on e-consultation and e-decision making, on the other hand, means that some of the countries have not incorporated e-consultation and e-decision making in their policymaking at all. As the stage of e-participation progresses, the mean value drops drastically from about 64 percent in the first stage to 31 percent in the second stage to 10 percent in the final stage of 2014. This indicates that countries have better utilized the initial e-information stage as compared to the more complex later

Table 5.1 Models for testing hypotheses

	Models 1 and 2	Model 3	Model 4
Purpose	Impact of technology, institutions, and their mediation effects on e-participation	Impact of technology, institutions, and their interaction on e-participation	Difference in impact of technology and institution factors across the three stages of e-information, e-consultation, and e-decision making
Hypotheses	H1, H2, H3	H4	H5
Dependent variable	E-participation (2012, 2014, and 2016)	E-participation (2012, 2014, and 2016)	E-information/ e-consultation/ e-decision making (2014, 2016, and 2018)
Explanatory variable	ICT infrastructure ICT affordability ICT skills ICT usage Political and regulatory Environment Political rights and civil liberties (2012, 2014, and 2016)	ICT infrastructure ICT affordability ICT skills ICT usage Political and regulatory Environment Political rights and civil liberties (2012, 2014, and 2016)	ICT infrastructure ICT affordability ICT skills ICT usage Political and regulatory Environment Political rights and civil liberties (2012, 2014, and 2016)
Control variables	National income (GDP per capita)	National income (GDP per capita)	National income (GDP per capita)
	Percentage of young in the population	Percentage of young in the population	Percentage of young in the population
	Urban population percentage	Urban population percentage	Urban population percentage
Analysis	CLPM	*T*-test; ANCOVA	Multivariate regression
Sample size (*N*)	143	143	143

stages and have scored the least on the top stage of e-decision making. Another important trend to note is that the mean value of e-participation score as well as the utilization across the three stages has consistently improved over the years. The utilization of ICTs for e-decision

Table 5.2 Data summary

Variable	Mean	SD	Minimum	Maximum
E-participation 2012	0.281	0.271	0	1
E-participation 2014	0.468	0.256	0.020	1
E-information 2014	63.688	27.086	7.41	100
E-consultation 2014	30.833	25.696	0	95.45
E-decision-making 2014	9.712	21.461	0	88.89
E-participation 2016	0.547	0.249	0.051	1
E-information 2016	65.178	25.093	8.8	100
E-consultation 2016	52.227	28.790	0	100
E-decision-making 2016	16.886	27.472	0	100
E-participation 2018	0.653	0.250	0.079	1
E-information 2018	73.473	20.843	23.33	100
E-consultation 2018	67.680	24.089	8.7	100
E-decision-making 2018	57.342	32.408	0	100

Table 5.3 Normality tests results for 2016 data

Variable	Pr(skewness)	Pr(kurtosis)	Adj. chi2(2)	Prob > chi2
E-participation	0.218	0.001	10.97	0.004
E-information	0.006	0.012	11.80	0.003
E-consultation	0.775	0.000	30.81	0.000
E-decision making	0.000	0.003	36.85	0.000
Political and regulatory environment	0.003	0.484	8.24	0.016
Political rights and civil liberties	0.080	0	38.54	0
Infrastructure	0.654	0.000	11.69	0.003
Affordability	0.002	0.213	9.63	0.008
Skills	0.001	0.103	11.68	0.003
Usage	0.054	0.005	10.24	0.006
GDP/capita	0	0	49.48	0
Percentage young	0	0	37.49	0
Urban population	0.165	0.002	10.21	0.006

making has seen the most drastic increase over the three surveys from a mean of 10 percent in 2014 to 57 percent in 2018. The mean e-participation score of all countries has gone up from 0.28 in 2012 to 0.65 in 2018.

The D'Agostino et al.'s (1990) skewness and kurtosis tests for normality were conducted, and the results are shown in Table 5.3 for the year 2016. The chi-squared probability tells that for each of these variables, the hypothesis that the variable is normally distributed can be rejected. The same holds true for the test results for 2012, 2014, and 2018. The skewness of a normal distribution is zero, and the first variable (e-participation) in 2016 has a negative value of –0.24 (as obtained by detailed summary not shown here) meaning it is negatively skewed. Negative skewness in this case indicates that there is higher concentration of countries toward lower e-participation scores. The data for all variables are either almost symmetrical (between –0.5 and 0.5 but not zero) or moderately skewed (range between –1 and –0.5 or between 0.5 and 1) except for gross domestic product (GDP) per capita and percentage young that are highly skewed with skewness values of 1.96 and 1.33, respectively. Kurtosis for a normal distribution is 3. The kurtosis for e-participation in 2016 is 2.15 (i.e., less than 3) for the variable e-participation, which indicates light tailed distributions (meaning less in the tails as compared to the rest of the distribution). GDP per capita and percentage young have kurtosis values of 6.97 and 7.36, respectively (that are above 3), representative of heavy tails, indicating large outliers.

Correlation Between the Variables

In the conceptual model, the political and regulatory environment and political rights and civil liberties are the two institutional resources. The ICT infrastructure, affordability, skills, and usage constitute the technology resources. Table 5.4 displays the correlation matrix between these variables for 2016. The technology variable of ICT infrastructure, skills,

Table 5.4 Correlation matrix for the explanatory variables in year 2016

	Political and regulatory environment	Political rights and civil liberties	Infrastructure	Affordability	Skills	Usage
Political and regulatory environment	1					
Political rights and civil liberties	0.453	1				
Infrastructure	0.697	0.579	1			
Affordability	0.233	0.327	0.477	1		
Skills	0.626	0.466	0.840	0.516	1	
Usage	0.849	0.504	0.897	0.483	0.834	1

and usage shows large (>0.5) correlation coefficient, and the variable "afford" shows a moderate (>0.3) correlation with the other technology variables. The two institutional variables of political rights and civil liberties and political and regulatory environment also show a moderate correlation of 0.45. With the only exception of ICT affordability, the other technology variables of ICT infrastructure, skills, and usage have moderate to large correlation coefficients with political and regulatory environment and political rights and civil liberties. Similar patterns are evident in other survey years as well. Thus, even though the technology and institutional variables show moderate to good convergent validity, the discriminant validity between the two constructs is poor. However, based on the previous discussion in Chapter 4, the measures for technology variables are distinct from the institutional variables.

The face validity of the political rights and civil liberties and political and regulatory environment as measures of institutions is convincing, and the same holds true for the face validity of the technology variables where all measures are related to ICT and, for the purpose of the current study, make sense to be considered as dimensions of technology. Furthermore, other studies (e.g., Åström et al., 2012; Gulati et al., 2014; Jho & Song, 2015) use these variables in the same manner such as political rights and civil liberties as institutional variables and price of telecommunication or number of internet connections as technology variables.

Mediation Analysis

Technology as Mediator

The CLPM model for technology as mediator of institutions has five exogenous variables: political rights and civil liberties, political and regulatory environment, national income, percentage young, and urban population percentage. There are four endogenous mediator variables: infrastructure (ICT availability), affordability, skills, and usage, and one endogenous variable (e-participation) in the model. Before analyzing the full mediation model, three preconditions of causation are established (Baron & Kenny, 1986), (1) the two independent variables of institutions – political and regulatory environment and political rights and civil liberties – predict e-participation longitudinally; (2) the four mediator variables of technology – infrastructure, affordability, skills, and usage – predict e-participation longitudinally; and (3) the two independent variables of institutions predict the four mediator variables of technology longitudinally.

These preconditions were tested for each of the institutional and technology variables combination. The preconditions tests reveal that both political and regulatory environment and political rights and civil liberties longitudinally predict e-participation. All the four technology variables of ICT infrastructure, affordability, skills, and usage also predict e-participation. These two preconditions satisfy the test for the first two hypothesis (H_1 and H_2) on the direct impact of institutional and technology variables on e-participation. The third precondition test results were established only for two of the four technology variables: political and regulatory environment predicts only ICT skills, and political rights and civil liberties predicts only ICT skills and ICT affordability. Thus, the final mediation analysis was conducted only for ICT skills and ICT affordability as mediators. Of these, the effect of political rights and civil liberties on e-participation with ICT affordability as a mediator did not come out to be statistically significant. The results for the two institutional variables on e-participation with ICT skills as a mediator are presented here.

Table 5.5 provides the direct, indirect, and total effects of the two institutional variables via the technology variable of ICT skills, analyzed in the final model. The indirect effects are of interest here as they represent the amount of mediation (Kenny, 2021). The results

Table 5.5 Mediation analysis results

	Coef.	*Std. coef.*
Direct effects		
Skills 2014 ≤		
Political and regulatory environment 2012	−0.095**	−0.070
Political rights and civil liberties 2012	0.035**	0.051
E-participation 2016 ≤		
Skills 2014	0.064***	0.322
Political and regulatory environment 2012	0.007	0.025
Political rights and civil liberties 2012	0.016*	0.119
Indirect effects		
E-participation 2016 ≤		
Political and regulatory environment 2012	−0.006**	−0.023
Political rights and civil liberties 2012	0.002*	0.017
Total effects		
E-participation 2016 ≤		
Skills 2014	0.064***	0.322
Political and regulatory environment 2012	0.001	0.002
Political rights and civil liberties 2012	0.018**	0.136

Significance at * $p ≤ 0.05$; ** $p ≤ 0.01$; *** $p ≤ 0.001$.

show that the technology variable of ICT skills mediates the effect of the institutions, as measured by the political and regulatory environment and political rights and civil liberties, on e-participation. The political and regulatory environment (2012) and political rights and civil liberties (2012) have a statistically significant ($p < 0.05$) indirect effect on e-participation (2016) via ICT skills (2014) as the mediator.

The standardized results in the last column indicate the change in the dependent variable given the explanatory variable, where both are measured in standard deviation units. The standardized coefficient (or beta weights) helps to compare the magnitude of impact for each variable. The political rights and civil liberties variable has a positive and significant indirect effect on e-participation: $\beta = 0.01653$, $z = 2.29$, $p < 0.05$. The political and regulatory environment, on the other hand, has a negative and statistically significant effect on e-participation: $\beta = -0.02259$, $z = -2.56$, $p < 0.05$. Note that the direct and total effect of political and regulatory environment on e-participation is positive. The negative value in indirect effect is because of the negative impact of political and regulatory environment on ICT skills. The current study uses the same World Economic Forum (WEF) survey data to measure both these variables. The negative indirect effect coefficient could be because of the fact that ICT skills scores in some countries have improved even when the political and regulatory environment scores of these countries has either not improved or deteriorated in the three years included in this study. This can be observed in the case of countries such as Chile, China, France, and Germany in the WEF surveys. The study also had three control variables in the model – national income, percentage of young (aged 18–24), and percentage of urban population in a country. None of the three control variables have a statistically significant effect on e-participation (2016).

Table 5.6 shows the results of the goodness of fit tests. The model meets four goodness of fit statistics (Hu & Bentler, 1999), namely, the comparative fit index (CFI = 0.972), the Tucker–Lewis index (TLI = 0.966), the standardized root mean squared residual (SRMR = 0.032), and the root mean squared error of approximation (RMSEA = 0.074 [90 percent confidence interval (CI) = 0.057, 0.090, $p = 0.011$]). The coefficient of determination (CD) is like the R square for a model and a value of 1 indicates a perfect fit. The model fails to pass the chi-square significance tests to reproduce the covariance matrix. Chi-square is sensitive to correlations, and larger correlations generally result in poorer fit (Kenny, 2020), which could be the case in current study. Therefore, the alternative tests of goodness of fit are also available in Stata.

Table 5.6 Goodness of fit test results

Fit statistic	Value	Description
Likelihood ratio		
chi2_ms(119)	211.146	Model vs. saturated
$p >$ chi2	0.000	
chi2_bs(144)	3396.598	Baseline vs. saturated
$p >$ chi2	0.000	
Population error		
RMSEA	0.074	Root mean squared error of approximation
90 percent CI, lower bound	0.057	
upper bound	0.090	
$p$close	0.011	Probability RMSEA $\leq$ 0.05
Information criteria		
AIC	11320.191	Akaike's information criterion
BIC	11447.593	Bayesian information criterion
Baseline comparison		
CFI	0.972	Comparative fit index
TLI	0.966	Tucker–Lewis index
Size of residuals		
SRMR	0.032	Standardized root mean squared residual
CD	1.000	Coefficient of determination

The study hypothesizes that the institutional variables of the political and regulatory environment and political rights and civil liberties and the technology variables of ICT infrastructure, affordability, skills, and usage of information and communication technology (ICT) influence the e-participation in a country positively. The findings in the preconditions test for the cross-lagged panel model support these hypotheses. Additionally, the study hypothesizes that technology mediates the institution's impact on e-participation. The findings support that ICT skills mediate the effect of political and regulatory environment and political rights and civil liberties on e-participation. The hypotheses H1a, b, c, and d for positive effect of technology on e-participation and H2a and b for positive effect of institutions on e-participation are supported by the preconditions test in mediation analysis. Hypothesis 3a is supported for ICT skills as the mediator for institutions' impact on e-participation.

Institution as Mediator

To test the model with institutions as mediator for technology variables' impact on e-participation, the precondition tests (Baron & Kenny,

1986) were performed. ICT infrastructure and usage are found to longitudinally predict the institutional variable of political and regulatory environment only. However, the mediation analysis fails to find a statistically significant indirect effect of either ICT infrastructure or usage on e-participation via political and regulatory environment. The test results fail to support the hypothesis that institutions mediate the influence of technology on e-participation. Hypothesis 3b for institutions as mediator is not supported.

Moderator Analysis

The current study wants to explore the influence of interaction effects of technology and institutions on the online participation. Following the study by Jho and Song (2015), first a *t*-test and then a three-way ANCOVA is conducted for assessing the interaction effects of technology and institutions on e-participation.

Two-Sample T-*Test*

To conduct the *t*-test, the 143 countries in the current study were categorized into two groups of high and low e-participation (i.e., those below and above the average score of all countries as in the study by Jho & Song, 2015). Next a two-sample *t*-test was run to compare the mean score of each explanatory and control variable between the two groups. The difference in means between the two group of countries in each year was statistically significant ($p < 0.05$) (see Rawat, 2020, for *t*-test results).

A boxplot of the e-participation by the various institutional and technology explanatory variables provides similar insight on the data distribution by median values. The countries are grouped as 0 and 1 by dividing them into two groups, where group 0 is below the mean value (i.e., lower score) and group 1 is above the mean value (i.e., higher score) for the particular explanatory variable. Figure 5.2 illustrates that the median value or the 50th percentile of e-participation in countries that are in group 0 is below those that are in group 1 for all explanatory variables. Thus, different levels of the explanatory variables do make a difference on e-participation. For example, the first boxplot in the set of graphs shows that the e-participation median score in 2012 is about 0.1 for countries with lower than average scores on political and regulatory environment, while it is 0.4 for countries with above average scores on political and regulatory environment.

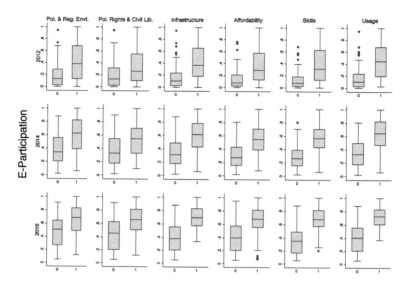

Figure 5.2 Box plots for e-participation in 2012, 2014, and 2016 by institutions and technology.

Note: 0 = countries below mean value of the explanatory variable;
1 = countries above mean value of the explanatory variable

Three-Way ANCOVA

A three-way ANCOVA is used where there is a need to understand the interaction effect between three independent variables on a continuous dependent variable. A three-way ANCOVA in the current study is analyzed for four separate interactions of explanatory variables (two institutional with one technical each) in each of the three years. The control variables are used in the analysis. Where analysis of variance (ANOVA) is augmented by allowing for the presence of one or more covariates in the analysis, it is called ANCOVA.

The countries are divided into two groups of above and below mean value for each explanatory variable (as in Jho & Song, 2015). The ANCOVA results indicate whether the two levels (low and high) of explanatory variables have any effect on e-participation and whether the interaction of the explanatory variables is significant. The study focuses on statistically significant interaction of institutions with each of the four technology variables. The interactions of two technology variables – ICT usage in 2014 and ICT infrastructure in 2016 – are statistically significant with the two institutional variables at 10 percent significance level ($p < 0.10$). The results of these two interactions are shown in Tables 5.7 and 5.8, respectively.

The moderator analysis shows that when the institutional variables of political and regulatory environment and political rights and civil liberties interact with ICT usage in 2014, their impact on e-participation is positively enhanced (partial sum of squares (SS) = 0.1125) and becomes statistically significant ($p < 0.1$) as compared to when they act independently. The F statistic and the p value corresponding to the interaction terms are significant at the 0.10 level of significance. The interaction effects of political and regulatory environment and political rights and civil liberties with ICT infrastructure in 2016 are also positive and significant (partial SS = 0.09843, $p < 0.1$). Thus, there is

Table 5.7 Interaction of the institutions with ICT usage in 2014

Dependent variable: e-participation

Source	SS	df	MS	F	Prob > F
Model	4.022	10	0.402	10.08	0.000
Political and regulatory environment	0.017	1	0.017	0.43	0.514
Political rights and civil liberties	0.007	1	0.007	0.17	0.681
Usage	0.478	1	0.478	11.97	0.001
Political and regulatory environment* Political rights and civil liberties*usage	0.113	1	0.113	2.82	0.095

R-squared = 0.433 (adj R-squared = 0.390); MS = mean square.

Table 5.8 Interaction of the institutions with ICT infrastructure in 2016

Dependent variable: e-participation

Source	SS	df	MS	F	Prob > F
Model	4.387	10	0.439	13.18	0.00
Political and regulatory environment	0.082	1	0.028	0.85	0.359
Political rights and civil liberties	0.048	1	0.048	1.43	0.233
Infrastructure	0.592	1	0.592	17.78	0.00
Political and regulatory environment* Political rights and civil liberties*infrastructure	0.098	1	0.098	2.96	0.088

R-squared = 0.500 (adj R-squared = 0.462); MS = mean square.

a statistically significant three-way interaction of institutions with ICT usage and ICT infrastructure.

The study hypothesizes that the technology variables of ICT infrastructure, affordability, skills, and usage moderate the impact of institutional variables of political and regulatory environment and political rights and civil liberties on e-participation. The ANCOVA results support the hypothesis for two technology variables of ICT infrastructure and usage in at least one of the three years. Hypothesis 4 for moderation is supported for interaction of institutions with two of the technology variables of ICT infrastructure and ICT usage. The *t*-test results, however, show that there is a statistically significant difference in means of the two groups of countries with low and high e-participation scores, for all explanatory variables.

Factors at Different Levels of E-Participation

Multivariate regression tests are used for testing the impact of factors across the three stages of e-participation in the three years. The results, as shown in Table 5.9, highlight political rights and civil liberties, ICT affordability, ICT usage as the variables that have statistically significant coefficients in at least one of the three years. Further tests were conducted to assess whether the difference in the coefficient of the variables across the three stages is significant. The test results for the null hypothesis that coefficients for ICT affordability in the equations with e-information, e-consultation, and e-decision making as the dependent variable are equal, or in other words, the difference is 0, is rejected for all the three years with $F(2, 133) = 6.36$, $p = 0.0023$ in 2014;

Table 5.9 Coefficients of significant factors across the three stages of e-participation

Variable	2014			2016			2018		
	EI	EC	ED	EI	EC	ED	EI	EC	ED
Political rights and civil liberties							2.19		2.8
ICT affordability	3.61			4.47	4.82			2.95	5.6
ICT usage	20.92	26.13	23.21	16.19	18.3		21.25	23.63	28.53

Note: Levels of e-participation, EI = e-information; EC = e-consultation; ED = e-decision making. Statistically significant coefficients at $p < 0.05$.

$F(2, 133) = 4.77$, $p = 0.0100$ in 2016; and $F(2, 133) = 4.07$, $p = 0.0193$ in 2018. However, it is only in 2018 that the ICT affordability coefficients consistently increase with each higher level of e-participation, with one unit change in ICT affordability associated with a 1.75 unit change in e-information (coefficient is statistically insignificant), a 2.95 unit change in e-consultation ($p = 0.03$), and a 5.60 unit change in e-decision-making stages ($p = 0.00$). The test results thus indicate that the ICT affordability coefficients for the three stages are significantly different and have an increasing effect as well as significance as e-participation progresses to higher levels. None of the tests for other variables resulted in statistically significant differences across the three stages in any of the three study years.

However, a point to note is that though multivariate regression requires the dependent variables to be at least moderately correlated with each other (University of California, Los Angeles [UCLA] Statistical Consulting Group, n.d.), some of the explanatory variables in the current study are also correlated. The explanatory variable of ICT usage is highly correlated with ICT infrastructure in all years, for example, in 2014, the ICT usage has a correlation coefficient (r) of 0.9126 with ICT infrastructure, 0.8174 with ICT skills, and 0.8556 with political and regulatory environment. ICT infrastructure is highly correlated with ICT skills and political and regulatory environment. Note that political and regulatory environment, ICT, infrastructure, and ICT usage are all from the same data source of WEF surveys, and their measures are exclusive.

The last hypothesis in the current study is that there is a difference in the technology and institutional variables at different levels of e-participation. The results show that ICT affordability, usage, and political rights and civil liberties are statistically significant, and their coefficients vary across the three stages. In 2016 and 2018, ICT affordability and usage display increasing and significant effect size, for at least two consecutive levels, indicating increasing impact for higher levels of e-participation. ICT affordability in 2018 is the only variable that has a statistically significant difference in effect size across the three stages and an increasing effect size as we progress from e-information to e-consultation and then e-decision making. Thus, hypothesis H5 is supported only for ICT affordability. ICT usage coefficients significantly impact all the three stages in 2018, with the effect size increasing at higher levels of e-participation, but the test results for the difference in the coefficients across the three stages are not significant. It is only in 2018 that the political rights and civil liberties significantly influences the e-information and e-consultation stage. However, it is not established that its effect size consistently increases toward higher levels as its impact on the e-consultation stage is not significant, nor are the test results for the difference in the coefficients across the three stages significant. A summary of all hypotheses test results across mediation, moderation, and different levels of e-participation is presented in Table 5.10.

Table 5.10 Summary of hypotheses test results

Hypotheses		Test result
Direct impact of technology	H1a): The availability of ICT infrastructure has a positive influence on e-participation. H1b): The affordability of ICT resources has a positive influence on e-participation. H1c): ICT skills have a positive influence on e-participation. H1d): Technology usage (enactment of technology) has a positive influence on e-participation.	All supported
Direct impact of institutions	H2a): Supporting political and regulatory environment in a country has a positive influence on the e-participation in that country. H2b): Political rights and civil liberties have a positive influence on e-participation.	All supported
Mediation analysis	H3a): Technology acts as a mediator for the institutions' impact on e-participation. H3b): Institutions act as a mediator for technology's impact on e-participation	Supported only for technology variable of ICT skills as mediator
Interaction of institutions and technology	H4: Technology and institutions interact to influence e-participation.	Supported for ICT usage in 2014 and ICT infrastructure in 2016; additionally, *t*-test supports significant difference in means of all explanatory variables between the two groups of countries with low and high e-participation.

Table 5.10 Cont.

Hypotheses		Test result
Factors at different levels of e-participation	H5: There is a difference in the technology and institutional resources for different levels of e-participation.	ICT affordability in 2018 has a significant and increasing effect size for higher levels of e-participation and the difference in effect size across the three stages is statistically significant.

References

Åström, J., Karlsson, M., Linde, J., & Pirannejad, A. (2012). Understanding the rise of e-participation in non-democracies: Domestic and international factors. *Government Information Quarterly, 29*(2), 142–150.

Baron, R. M., & Kenny, D. A. (1986). The moderator–mediator variable distinction in social psychological research: Conceptual, strategic, and statistical considerations. *Journal of Personality and Social Psychology, 51*(6), 1173–1182. https://doi.org/10.1037/0022-3514.51.6.1173.

D'Agostino, R. B., Belanger, A., & D'Agostino, R. B., Jr. (1990). A suggestion for using powerful and informative tests of normality. *The American Statistician, 44*(4), 316–321.

Gulati, G., Williams, C. B., & Yates, D. J. (2014). Predictors of on-line services and e-participation: A cross-national comparison. *Government Information Quarterly, 3*(1), 526–533.

Hu, L., & Bentler, P. M. (1999). Cutoff criteria for fit indexes in covariance structure analysis: Conventional criteria versus new alternatives. *Structural Equation Modeling, 6*, 1–55.

Jho, W., & Song, K. J. (2015). Institutional and technological determinants of civil e-participation: Solo or duet? *Government Information Quarterly, 3*(2), 488–495.

Kenny, D. A. (2020). Measuring model fit. Retrieved from http://davidakenny. net/cm/fit.htm. Accessed on June 12, 2021.

Kenny, D. A. (2021). Mediation. Retrieved from http://davidakenny.net/cm/ mediate.htm. Accessed on June 12, 2021.

Rawat, P. (2020). A policy feedback and socio-technical approach to e-participation (PFSTEP): A cross-national analysis of technology and institutions to explain e-participation. *Journal of Information Technology & Politics*. doi:10.1080/19331681.2020.1839621.

Scholl, H. J. (2005). Organizational transformation through e-government: Myth or reality? In M. A. Wimmer, R. Traunmüller, Å. Grönlund, & K. V. Andersen (Eds.), *Electronic government*. EGOV 2005. Lecture Notes in Computer Science, Vol. 3591. Berlin: Springer.

UCLA Statistical Consulting Group. (n.d.). Multivariate regression. Institute for Digital Research and Education [IDRE]. Retrieved from https://stats.idre. ucla.edu/stata/dae/multivariate-regression-analysis/. Accessed on January 1, 2018.

Ullman, J. (2006). Structural equation modeling: Reviewing the basics and moving forward. *Journal of Personality Assessment*, *87*(1), 35–50.

Wooldridge, J. (2000). *Introductory econometrics: A modern approach.* Cincinnati, OH: South-Western College.

6 Implications and Outlook

Evaluating the Policy Feedback and Socio-Technical Approach to E-Participation (PFSTEP) Model

The first research question asked in the beginning of the study was what factors explain the difference in the degree of e-participation across countries? Based on the PFSTEP, the model conceptualized in the current study, the impact of technology and institutional resources on e-participation was statistically analyzed in multiple ways using panel data. The analysis suggested that both the institutional variables of political and regulatory environment and political rights and civil liberties had a direct longitudinal impact on e-participation. All four technology variables of ICT infrastructure, affordability, skills, and usage also had a significant longitudinal direct impact on e-participation. The results also supported the role of these ICT skills as the mediator for institutional variables of political and regulatory environment and political rights and civil liberties. Further, the moderation analysis confirmed that the interaction of ICT infrastructure and usage with the two institutional variables had a positive and significant impact on e-participation. The t-test results suggested that the group of countries that have higher than average e-participation scores also had higher than average scores on all the six explanatory variables and the three control variables of national income, percentage young, and percentage urban population. Further, based on the test results, neither of the two institutional variables mediated the effect of technology on e-participation, thus failing to support the hypothesis that technology impacts e-participation indirectly via institutions. This finding further validates the role of institutions as antecedents to technology (instead of vice versa) for e-participation. This can also be an indication that the technology resources are yet to create a sufficiently strong feedback loop to

DOI: 10.4324/9781003164326-6

generate a statistically significant impact on institutions to promote (or discourage) e-participation.

Higher scores of political rights and civil liberties for a country means that the people in those countries enjoy pluralism, free and fair electoral processes, freedom of belief and expression, rights to associate and organize, and better rule of law and functioning of government (Freedom House, 2014) leading to improved opportunities for political participation. The election rights and rights of equality foster interpretive resources of participation leading to better skills and more ICT usage that improves e-participation. Similarly, better political and regulatory environments in a country mean effective law-making bodies and ICT laws, protection of intellectual property, lower rates of software piracy, an efficient legal system, an independent judiciary, and better enforcement of contracts (World Economic Forum [WEF], 2016). These conditions encourage the spread and usage of ICT resources for online participation. For example, an efficient judiciary promotes effective contract enforcement that leads to expansion of trade (Cusatelli & Giacalone, 2014) and free economic activity, leading to more competition and thus improved and more affordable ICT infrastructure (Gulati et al., 2014) that improves e-participation. The laws relating to ICTs, intellectual property protection, and countermeasures for software piracy promote usage of ICT by individuals as well as businesses that is reflected in innovations, patents, ICT absorption, and business to consumer internet use (refer to the Appendix for WEF variables and measures). The availability and quality of government online services, which is a measure of ICT usage, is positively impacted by the presence of competitive political parties and strong opposition, effective law-making bodies and laws relating to ICTs, as well as better scores in contract enforcement.

Institutions have a statistically significant indirect effect when mediated by technology variables of ICT skills. This is a significant finding of this study. Institutions are the antecedents to technology resources and impact e-participation via ICT skills. Previous studies did not find either a significant (e.g., Jho & Song, 2015) or a positive (e.g., Gulati et al., 2014) impact of freedom or democratic institutions on e-participation. Looking at the direct impact of institutions on e-participation using cross-sectional data, as in past studies, it may appear that the institutional variables are not important. However, by using panel data, the current study negates the previous findings, and the results in this book support the longitudinal direct impact of institutions, the role of institutions as precursors to technology's impact on e-participation, and the interactions of institutions with technology having a positive and significant impact on e-participation. Previous cross-country studies have not considered the mediator aspect of technology and instead have focused on the interaction between technology and institutions. The path analysis in this study has highlighted this aspect of institutions as predecessors and ICT skills as the mediator for institutions' impact on e-participation.

Higher ICT skills imply better quality education systems, including math and science education, and adult literacy rates (measures of ICT skills) leading to improved e-participation. The Dutch are one of the most technology savvy countries (WEF, 2016), and the Netherlands has consistently scored very high on e-participation scales despite low affordability of ICTs. In a survey-based research study, computer or internet skills are assessed asking questions about whether the individual has used email, sent attachments (Best & Krueger, 2005), and an individual's frequency of internet use (Anduiza et al., 2010). However, an evaluation of either computer or online skills is missing in the cross-country analysis literature of e-participation, probably due to the lack of such data at national level. Education is typically used as a variable and measured using an enrollment ratio or literacy rate in the cross-country models, for example, Gulati et al. (2014) measure education level in a country using gross enrollment ratio and adult literacy rate in United Nations' (UN) education index (UN, 2007) and find that higher levels of education have a substantial effect on a nation's e-participation capabilities. Others (Åström et al., 2012; Jho & Song, 2015) use the Human Development Index (HDI), which is a composite index of income, education, and lifespan that does not specifically provide any insight on the unique impact of ICT skills on e-participation. Our study selects the WEF's ICT skills as a measure. In the absence of data on computer and internet skills at national level, WEF's ICT skills are a better measure than the HDI because they do not conflate health and income aspects with education. At the same time, WEF's ICT skills are a better measure than the education levels used in Gulati et al. (2014) because, apart from education levels, they use survey data of countries on questions related to the ability of the educational system to meet the needs of a competitive economy and the quality of math and science education in a country (WEF, 2016).

The second research question posed in the study was: do the factors differ in their influence on e-information, e-consultation, and e-decision-making levels? As per the UN's (2018) survey, even though overall countries have progressed on e-participation, e-decision making is still a challenge even for developed countries. Only a few studies (e.g., Krishnan et al., 2013) have explored the differences across the three levels of e-participation. The results in the current study show that the magnitudes of ICT affordability are significant for at least two consecutive levels and consistently increase from lower to higher levels of e-participation in 2018 with the difference across these levels being significant. The effect size of ICT affordability is least in the first level of e-information, and its magnitude increases in the higher levels of e-consultation and e-decision making. Thus, every unit change in ICT affordability has a greater change in e-decision making than in e-consultation, which in turn is more than the change in e-information.

We now turn to the effect of these variables with examples from a few countries. UN's latest e-participation survey (UN, 2020) shows that countries like India and Indonesia are low on technology as compared to Ireland and Israel, and yet they have a "very high" e-participation index (EPI). In fact, their EPI is as good as that of Ireland ("very high") and even better than that of Israel ("high") despite the fact that both India and Indonesia score far lower on technology (UN, 2020) as compared to the latter two countries. The telecom infrastructure scores for India and Indonesia, as well as the percentage of people using the internet, are less than half as compared to Ireland and Israel. The broadband subscriptions percentage in India and Indonesia are at 1.34 percent and 3.32 percent as compared to close to 30 percent in Ireland and Israel. India advanced from "low" EPI in 2012 to "high" EPI in 2014 and then attained and maintained a "very high" EPI 2016 onward. Indonesia, on the other hand, advanced comparatively gradually from "low" EPI in 2012 and 2014 to "middle" EPI in 2016, "high" in 2018, and then "very high" in 2020. So how did these countries manage to advance to high scores on EPI? What aspects of technology and institutions were focused on? Both India and Indonesia have high mobile subscription percentages, and it is this technology that these countries are harnessing. India's cost for an Android phone halved in 2012 leading to increasing ownership of mobile phones (UN, 2014), and the country crossed a major milestone of 1 billion mobile phone subscriptions in 2015. The Indian government created the National Optical Fiber Network in 2011 connecting 250,000 villages with fixed-line broadband (UN, 2020). India and Indonesia rank second and third, respectively, in the biggest share of internet users in Asia as of May 2020, after China (Statista, 2021). On the ICT skills front, India has one of the largest education systems in the world, next only to the United States and China (Tyagi & Singh, 2015). India's National Mission on Education through Information and Communication Technology (ICT) intends to empower those who are left out of the digital revolution so that they can join the mainstream knowledge economy. The Digital India program, launched in 2015, aimed at universal digital literacy, among other goals, and has enrolled millions for digital literacy and provided internet connectivity to village governing bodies (Digital India, 2020). Indonesia similarly launched several programs since 2014 promoting ICT hard and soft skills, including an e-commerce road map in 2017 that has a substantial focus on ICT generic and specialist skill development (World Bank, 2018).

None of these technological advances of ICT availability, affordability, and skills could be possible without government policies. On the institutional resources front, India maintained its Freedom House scores on political rights and civil liberties in 2012, 2014, and 2016 at the same level (Free), while Indonesia declined to "partly free" status in 2014. However, Indonesia's political and regulatory environment scores improved between 2012 and 2016. One of the major initiatives of India that finds recurring mention in the UN surveys is financial inclusion, and this, along with many of the Digital India initiatives, was made possible and ride on the digital identity platform that India created under its Unique Identity (UID) program (see Rawat & Morris, 2019, for more on UID). The UID program started enrolling in 2010 and provided digital identity to more than 1.2 billion people by 2018 and facilitates government, public, and business interactions online at various levels (UN, 2020). Of the few lower middle-income countries that adopted Open Government Data (OGD) initiatives were India and Indonesia (UN, 2014). Indonesia started to show substantial improvement in the provision of government services online in the 2018 survey (UN, 2018). This discussion exhibits how the explanatory factors in the PFSTEP model varied alongside e-participation in the context of India and Indonesia.

ICT affordability is the technology resource that shows an increasing effect size from lower to higher levels of e-participation. E-information comprises one-way communication technology for which a website may suffice, but e-consultation requires the availability of online tools that facilitate two-way communication. Larger data transfers, remote access, and video chats require more data and bandwidth consumption, adding to the cost of ICT. E-decision-making systems, such as e-voting, require systems that meet several complex requirements of the anonymity of voters, accuracy and reliability of processes, and security against cybersecurity issues. These are complex requirements, not a linear addition of tools or information to existing ones, and these are the dimensions that countries struggle most with. Only a few countries, such as Estonia, have used e-voting on a national scale such as for parliamentary elections. An example of the role of ICT affordability is in a country like India that had low e-participation, especially e-decision-making scores that shot up in 2016. In 2015, India's largest mobile network operator was launched that brought in huge fall in tariff rates and reduction of data charges. India ranks among cheapest in mobile data and fixed-line broadband prices in the world (Cable. co.uk, 2021).

Many of the countries that are high on the EPI also have high tariffs on mobiles and broadband, for example, the Netherlands and Luxembourg. The Netherlands, one of the consistently top performers in e-participation, has high mobile tariffs and broadband prices that continue to rise (WEF, 2016). The United States has the least expensive broadband package among high-income countries, but it is slipping in its ranking on the international internet bandwidth per user as the race grows (WEF, 2016). However, if we assess as a percentage of income, then the UN e-government survey of 2018 reports that the European citizens spend only 0.63 percent of their income on mobile broadband subscription. At the same time, Oceania spends 4.34 percent, Americans 2.5 percent, Asians 8.77 percent, while African citizens spend 13.49 percent of their income on mobile services. Yet, according to the UN, Europeans have the largest broadband subscription at 80.46 percent and the Africans have the least at 27.84 percent. Europeans also have the highest percentage utilization of ICTs across all stages with the e-decision-making stage score at 0.78 as compared to 0.54 for the Americas, 0.53 for Asia, 0.26 for Oceania, and 0.22 for Africa. Europeans spend the smallest percentage of their income on mobile broadband subscription (most affordable mobile broadband subscription), yet they have highest percentage of population subscribed to broadband and the highest proportion of countries with very high EPI levels. In recent years, ICT access and affordability has improved due to the access to mobile phones (UN, 2018).

The Digital Divide

Our study emphasizes the role of institutions in providing technical resources that improves e-participation. E-participation depends on these resources. However, resources are unequally distributed leading to unequal participation (Verba, 1996). Unequal participation has been raised as an issue even in the offline or traditional participation literature (Arnstein, 1969; Lijphart, 1997; Norris, 2001; Verba, 1996). The digital divide exacerbates the gap in society and restricts the ability of ICT to improve the functioning of democracy (West, 2005).

The current study uses the dimensions of ICT infrastructure, meaning the availability of ICTs, as well as ICT affordability, skills, and usage, and by doing so evaluates various dimensions of the digital divide and its impact on e-participation. The International Telecommunication Union (ITU, 2020) reports that 72 percent of the world's urban population and only 38 percent of its rural population had internet access in 2019. Further, in Africa, only 28 percent of urban and only 6.3 percent of the rural population had internet access (ITU, 2020). Scholars have warned that the inequalities in ICT access are closely linked to the inequalities traditionally observed in political participation (Vicente & Novo, 2014). Due to higher cost of broadband, those using it are richer, more educated, and in urban areas (Leigh and Atkinson, 2001). Affordability of ICTs creates a divide between rich and poor both across, as well as within countries. In their seminal study, Van Dijk and Hacker (2003) argued that the digital divide concept is shifting from possession of computers and network connections to gaps in digital skills and usage. The findings in the current book highlight that an important dimension of digital divide – ICT skills – acts as a mediator for institutions' impact on e-participation. ICT skills are the technical resource through which the political and regulatory environment and political rights and civil liberties in a country improve e-participation. At the same time, ICT infrastructure and usage strengthen the impact of these institutions on e-participation. ICT affordability is significant in determining the level of online public participation and has greater effect size on higher levels of e-participation. This study has thus highlighted the various dimensions of digital divide that are significant for e-participation, and how they impact e-participation. The current study augments the digital divide literature by adding the role of institutions as antecedents to technology factors and by highlighting the role of various technology dimensions in e-participation.

The discussion of the digital divide is spread across a range of technologies that can be used for inclusion. The findings of a study in South Africa suggests that socially excluded groups are approving, as well as capable, of using mobile technology as a platform for e-participation, thus debunking the argument that digital skills are at the heart of digital divide (Ochara & Mawela, 2015). The study emphasizes that mobile devices should be adopted and adapted for e-participation, and computer, multimedia, and computer-mediated literacy should be embraced in all spheres including education as well as workplaces for e-participation (Ochara & Mawela, 2015). Mobile phones have improved the access and affordability of ICTs, but new "multiple digital divides" have emerged with respect to speed and quality of those devices, high-speed broadband access, digital literacy to use the new devices, and the ability to take complete advantage of the ICT technology (UN, 2018, p. 34).

Despite the benefits of mobile connectivity in bridging access gaps, there is an increasing realization on the importance of fixed lines for inclusion of all, for example, India's National Optical Fiber Network that was discussed in a previous section of this chapter (UN, 2018). Emerging technologies of artificial intelligence, machine learning, and big data and analytics are considered to offer a bright future for social inclusion (UN, 2018). However, several issues of biases in this front have become a significant area of study (e.g., Gianfrancesco et al., 2018; Mayson, 2019). At the same time, cloud-based services and data localization regulations along with the concerns of cybersecurity are creating new digital divides of restricted access to government information such as for migrants (UN, 2018).

Contributions to Practice

The most novel contribution of this study is to establish the role of institutions as precursor to technology in promoting e-participation in a country. Freedom House (2017) reported that for 11 consecutive years (2005–2016), the number of countries that have seen a deterioration in political rights and civil liberties has outnumbered the countries that have shown progress on these indices. At the same time, the access to information using ICTs has increased in the past two decades with the number of internet users increasing from one billion in 2005 to three billion in 2014 (Internet Live Stats, 2017). The current study emphasizes that the growth in technology resources has to be supported by the institutional resources for a positive effect on e-participation. The presence of strong institutional resources such as political rights and civil liberties and regulatory support such as ICT laws, effective dispute settlement, independent judiciary, and effectiveness of law-making bodies will encourage the adoption of ICT infrastructure for the purposes of e-participation. Luxembourg, despite poor affordability of ICTs (WEF, 2016), is high on e-participation. One of the parameters that it excels is in ICT laws, such as consumer protection and e-commerce (WEF, 2016). Slovakia showed a large increase in e-participation scores from 0.5424 in 2016 to 0.809 in 2018. WEF (2016) reports that, apart from procuring advanced technologies for improving government efficiency, the Slovak government is showing visible signs of improvement in ICT laws, effectiveness of the legislature, and independence of its judiciary.

The moderation analysis has suggested that the group of countries that have higher e-participation also have higher levels of political rights and civil liberties, political and regulatory environment, ICT availability, affordability, skills, and usage. The availability of ICT is important, but not sufficient, for e-participation. Countries need to develop various aspects of technology, specifically those that facilitate e-participation. As previously discussed, despite an extensive mobile network coverage and extremely competitive telecommunication market, India had low e-participation scores. Since India launched a policy on Digital India and developed a platform for sharing and commenting on policies in 2014 that promoted ICT usage by government agencies for public participation, its e-participation score rose significantly in 2016. Apart from that, India has some of the least expensive mobile data and broadband prices in the world (Cable.co.uk, 2021). Having ICT available, at affordable rates, developing necessary skills, and promoting its use across the sectors of government, business, and society are all important dimension of technology resources that facilitate e-participation.

The current study draws attention to facets like ICT skills and usage in countries for promoting e-participation. Both the United States and the United Kingdom provide favorable business environments that lead to digitized business sector and the public sector's effective use of digital platforms for public service delivery and public participation (WEF, 2016). Further, UK government and businesses are top performers in use of internet and technology (WEF, 2016). Citizen engagement is fundamentally a knowledge-building exercise with profoundly positive benefits to policy development (Lukensmeyer & Torres, 2006). In the current study, ICT skills have emerged as dominant factors with significant positive impact on e-participation and are a reflection of knowledge building. ICT skills are an important factor that have a direct positive influence and mediate institutional resources in promoting e-participation.

Contributions to Theory

The current study uses a novel combination of policy feedback and a socio-technical approach to develop a conceptual model of e-participation. The policy feedback has not been utilized much in previous studies of online participation. The theories of policy feedback, structuration, and technology-in-practice lens have been used in a novel way in this study to evaluate the difference in e-participation across countries.

Mettler (2002) argues that the policies provide citizens the capacity to participate by providing resources. Citizen's understanding of their roles in society and to participate are influenced by the laws and administration (Mettler, 2002; Mettler & Sorrelle, 2018). The current study contributes to the policy feedback theory by conducting a cross-national analysis to explore the indirect effect of institutional resources on e-participation via technology. Previous cross-country studies have not looked at this aspect of institutions but rather focused on interactions between technology and institutions and/or found insignificant direct impacts of institutions on e-participation. The path analysis in the current study has indicated that institutions engender technology resources to promote e-participation. By finding support for technology as a mediator and rejecting the role of institutions as a mediator, the findings of the current study help infer more emphatically that the government policies create resources that promote public participation. Further, some previous studies highlighted that availability of infrastructure does not improve users' intention to participate and explained this phenomenon using demand side or users' side factors (Choi & Kim, 2012; Yao & Murphy, 2007; Zolotov et al., 2018). The policy feedback theory used in the current study may provide a possible alternative explanation from the supply side by emphasizing the interpretive effects of the political and regulatory environment and political rights and civil liberties in engendering e-participation. The current study also supports Orlikowski's (2000) technology in practice theory by finding a significant effect of ICT usage as a moderator to improve e-participation.

The current study supports that a country's political and regulatory environment has a significant direct and indirect effect on e-participation. This is consistent with the past cross-national study on e-participation by Gulati et al. (2014), whose findings reveal that professional practices of public administration and government performance improve e-participation. On the other hand, the current study also finds support for the hypothesis that previous literature is unable to corroborate. By using panel data and cross-lagged panel model (CLPM), this study finds that political rights and civil liberties influence e-participation directly, as well as indirectly, via ICT skills. Gulati et al. (2014), who measure democratic political culture using a composite scale including Freedom House scores in combination with other indicators of democracy, did not find support for a democratic political structure's effect on the extent of a country's e-participation. The same nonconforming results for the democracy scores are reported in the study by Åström et al. (2012), who argue that the results are such because of the rise in e-participation among nondemocratic countries and not because of a negative trend among the democratic countries.

This book brings together theories of policy process and information technology in one conceptual model for analysis. The importance of resources for participation, even though common and extensively used in public participation and e-participation literature, is under various labels such as resources approach, resources effect of policy feedback theory, and resources mobilization. The current study shows that in the development of all these approaches, there is a common literature, such as that of Verba et al. (1993) and Lazarsfeld et al. (1948) that ties these together. The socio-technical literature referring to scholars such as Giddens' (1984) work and Orlikowski's (2000) practice lens is used in the current study with the policy feedback effect in one model to argue the interconnection between technology and institutions. In the current study, the existing policies in a country are seen as the ones that shape technology and institutional resources in a country, and these resources provide a complex, intertwined context in which the human action of e-participation takes place.

Directions for Future Research

The current study has highlighted the complex and intertwined nature of the technology and resource variables and their impact on e-participation. The study used multiple dimensions of technology and institutions to provide better understanding and actionable feedback. Future studies can refine the model by deconstructing each variable into further discrete components that are used to measure the variable. For example, instead of using a composite measure of ICT usage, it might be useful to study the impact of either government and/or individual usage on e-participation. This will aid in creating a list of discrete actionable items in the technology and institutions side. However, doing so will also increase the number of parameters to be assessed in a model, requiring more data points to evaluate such data. The second course to take in future studies is to analyze different path models using these and other variables. Future studies can also analyze the PFSTEP model at lower levels of government. Further, a pool of qualitative studies can be developed using the institutional and technology factors in PFSTEP that will enhance the understanding and substantiate the findings of how these factors improve e-participation. A comparative study using this model can further substantiate the model's reliability. Apart from this, information privacy and cybersecurity in e-participation applications and processes are evolving areas of study that are yet to be adopted rigorously in the social science domain. Security such as that of e-voting applications against threats of availability, integrity, and confidentiality of applications and content by malicious online behavior may impact adoption and use of e-voting mechanisms (Zissis & Lekkas, 2011). A challenge for future studies is to select the variables to keep or add, and the ones to drop from a study, given the vast number of variables that have been analyzed in public participation literature – both online and offline. It will be helpful to categorize the sets of variables, for example, technology and institutions in the current study, evaluate their impacts both quantitatively and qualitatively, and create a list of the most influential explanatory variables for e-participation at different levels of government.

References

Anduiza, E., Gallego, A., & Cantijoch, M. (2010). Online political participation in Spain: The impact of traditional and internet resources. *Journal of Information Technology & Politics, 7*(4), 356–368.

Arnstein, S. (1969). A ladder of citizen participation. *Journal of the American Institution of Planners, 35*(4), 216–224.

Åström, J., Karlsson, M., Linde, J., & Pirannejad, A. (2012). Understanding the rise of e-participation in non-democracies: Domestic and international factors. *Government Information Quarterly, 29*(2), 142–150.

Best, S., & Krueger, J. (2005). Analyzing the representativeness of internet political participation. *Political Behavior, 27*(2), 183–216.

Cable.co.uk. (2021). Worldwide data pricing. Retrieved from www.cable.co.uk/mobiles/worldwide-data-pricing/. Accessed on April 24, 2021.

Choi, S. O., & Kim, B. C. (2012). Voter intention to use e-voting technologies: Security, technology acceptance, election type, and political ideology. *Journal of Information Technology & Politics, 9* (4), 433–452. doi:10.1080/19331681.2012.710042.

Cusatelli, C., & Giacolone, M. (2014). Evaluation indices of the judicial system and ICT developments in civil procedure. *Procedia Economics and Finance, 17*(2014), 113–120.

Digital India. (2020). Retrieved from www.digitalindia.gov.in. Accessed on April 5, 2021.

Freedom House. (2014). Freedom in the world 2014. Retrieved from https://freedomhouse.org/sites/default/files/FIW2014%20Booklet.pdf. Accessed on June 3, 2021.

Freedom House. (2017). Freedom in the world 2017. Retrieved from https://freedomhouse.org/sites/default/files/FH_FIW_2017_Report_Final.pdf. Accessed on June 3, 2021.

Gianfrancesco, M. A., Tamang, S., Yazdany, J., & Schmajuk, G. (2018). Potential biases in machine learning algorithms using electronic health record data. *JAMA Internal Medicine, 178*(11), 1544–1547. doi:10.1001/jamainternmed.2018.3763.

Giddens, A. (1984). *The constitution of society: Outline of the theory of structuration.* Cambridge: Polity Press.

Gulati, G., Williams, C. B., & Yates, D. J. (2014). Predictors of on-line services and e-participation: A cross-national comparison. *Government Information Quarterly, 3*(1), 526–533. doi:10.1016/j.giq.2014.07.005.

International Telecommunication Union (ITU). (2020). Measuring digital development: Facts and figures, 2020. Retrieved from www.itu.int/en/ITU-D/Statistics/Documents/facts/FactsFigures2020.pdf. Accessed on February 16, 2021.

Internet Live Stats. (2017). Internet users. Retrieved from www.internetlivestats.com/internet-users/. Accessed on June 23, 2021.

Jho, W., & Song, K. J. (2015). Institutional and technological determinants of civil e-participation: Solo or duet? *Government Information Quarterly, 3*(2), 488–495. doi:10.1016/j.giq.2015.09.003.

Krishnan S., Teo T. S. H., & Lim J. (2013). E-participation and e-government maturity: A global perspective. In Y. K. Dwivedi, H. Z. Henriksen, D. Wastell, & R. De' (Eds.), *Grand successes and failures in IT public and private sectors*. TDIT 2013. IFIP Advances in Information and Communication Technology, Vol. 402. Berlin: Springer. https://doi.org/10.1007/978-3-642-38862-0_26.

Lazarsfled, P., Berelson, B., & Gaudet, H. (1948). *The people's choice: How the voter makes up his mind in a presidential campaign*. New York, NY: Columbia University Press.

Leigh, A., & Atkinson, R. (2001). *Clear thinking on the digital divide*. Washington, DC: Progressive Policy Institute.

Lijphart, A. (1997). Unequal participation: Democracy's unresolved dilemma. *The American Political Science Review, 91*(1), 1–14.

Lukensmeyer, C. J., & Torres, L. H. (2006). Public deliberation: A manager's guide to citizen engagement. Retrieved from www.whitehouse.gov/files/documents/ostp/opengov_inbox/ibmpubdelib.pdf. Accessed on January 24, 2016.

Mayson, S. G. (2019). Bias in, bias out. *The Yale Law Journal, 128*(8), 2218.

Mettler, S. (2002). Bringing the state back in to civic engagement: Policy feedback effects of the G.I. Bill for World War II veterans. *American Political Science Review, 96*(2), 351–365.

Mettler, S., & Sorrelle, M. (2018). Policy feedback theory. In C. M. Weible & P. A. Sabatier (Eds.), *Theories of the policy process* (4th ed., pp. 103–134). Boulder, CO: Westview Press.

Norris, P. (2001). *Digital divide: Civic engagement, information poverty, and the internet worldwide*. Cambridge: Cambridge University Press.

Ochara, N. M., & Mawela, T. (2015). Enabling social sustainability of e-participation through mobile technology. *Information Technology for Development, 21*(2), 205–228. https://doi-org.proxy.lib.odu.edu/10.1080/02681102.2013.833888.

Orlikowski, W. J. (2000). Using technology and constituting structures: A practice lens for studying technology in organizations. *Organization Science, 4*, 404.

Rawat, P., & Morris, J. C. (2019). The global and the local: Tracing the trajectory of the largest biometric identity program: India's biometric identity program. *Politics & Policy, 47*(2), 1066–1094. doi:10.1111/polp.12334.

Statista. (2021). Countries with the biggest share of internet users in Asia as of May 2020, by country. Retrieved from www.statista.com/statistics/272358/distribution-of-internet-users-in-asia-pacific-by-country/. Accessed on April 2, 2021.

Tyagi, R., & Singh, R. (2015). Status of ICT in education and support of Govt. of India. *International Journal of Engineering Research and General Science, 3*(1), 1323–1332.

United Nations (UN). (2007). *Human development report 2007/2008*. New York, NY: Palgrave Macmillan.

United Nations (UN). (2014). E-government survey 2014. Retrieved from https://publicadministration.un.org/egovkb/en-us/Reports/UN-E-Government-Survey-2014. Accessed on June 3, 2021.

United Nations (UN). (2018). E-government survey 2018. Retrieved from https://publicadministration.un.org/egovkb/en-us/Reports/UN-E-Government-Survey-2018. Accessed on June 3, 2021.

United Nations (UN). (2020). E-government survey 2020. Retrieved from https://publicadministration.un.org/egovkb/en-us/Reports/UN-E-Government-Survey-2020. Accessed on June 3, 2021.

Van Dijk, J. A. G. M., & Hacker, K. (2003). The digital divide as a complex and dynamic phenomenon. *Information Society, 19*, 315–326. doi:10.1080/01972240309487.

Verba, S. (1996). The citizen as respondent: Sample surveys and American democracy. *American Political Science Review, 90*, 1–7.

Verba, S., Schlozman, K., Brady, H., & Nie, N. H. (1993). Citizen activity: Who participates? What do they say? *American Political Science Review, 87*(2), 303–318.

Vicente, M. R., & Novo, A. (2014). An empirical analysis of e-participation. The role of social networks and e-government over citizens' online engagement. *Government Information Quarterly, 31*(3), 379–387.

West, D. (2005). *Digital government technology and public-sector performance* (Safari tech books online ed.). Princeton, NJ: Princeton University Press.

World Bank. (2018). Preparing ICT Skills for digital economy: Indonesia within the ASEAN context. Retrieved from https://blogs.worldbank.org/sites/default/files/preparing_ict_skills_for_digital_economy-revised_7mar2018.pdf. Accessed on April 5, 2021.

World Economic Forum (WEF). (2016). Networked readiness index. Retrieved from www3.weforum.org/docs/GITR2016/GITR_2016_full%20report_final.pdf. Accessed on June 3, 2021.

Yao, Y., & Murphy, L. (2007). Remote electronic voting systems: An exploration of voters' perceptions and intention to use. *European Journal of Information Systems, 16*, 106–120.

Zissis, D., & Lekkas, D. (2011). Securing e-government and e-voting with an open cloud computing architecture. *Government Information Quarterly, 28*(2), 239–251.

Zolotov, M. N., Oliveira, T., & Casteleyn, S. (2018). E-participation adoption models research in the last 17 years: A weight and meta-analytical review. *Computers in Human Behavior, 81*, 350–365.

Appendix: List of Variables, Measures, and Their Data Sources

Group	Variable	Measures	Source
Dependent variables	E-participation	E-participation score	UN e-participation survey scores
	E-information	E-information percentage	
	E-consultation	E-consultation percentage	
	E-decision making	E-decision-making percentage	
Technology	ICT availability	Electricity production (kWh/capita), mobile network coverage (as a percentage of population), international internet bandwidth (kb/s per user), and secure internet servers/ million population.	NRI – WEF
	ICT affordability	Cellular and fixed broadband internet tariffs, and internet and telephony competition	NRI – WEF
	ICT skills	Quality of educational system (1–7 best), quality of math and science education (1–7 best), secondary education gross enrolment rate (percentage), adult literacy rate, (percentage)	NRI – WEF

Group	Variable	Measures	Source
	ICT usage – individual/ businesses/ government	• Individual usage – mobile phone subscriptions/ 100 population, individuals using internet, percentage households w/ personal computer, percentage households w/ internet access, percentage fixed broadband internet subs/100 population, mobile broadband subs/100 population, use of virtual social networks (1–7 best) • Business usage – firm-level technology absorption, capacity for innovation, PCT patent applications per million population, ICT use for business-to-business transactions, business-to-consumer internet use, extent of staff training. • Government usage – importance of ICTs to government vision (1–7 best), government Online Service Index, 0–1 (best), government success in ICT promotion (1–7 best)	NRI- WEF
Institutions	Political and regulatory environment	Effectiveness of law-making bodies, 1–7 (best); Laws relating to ICTs, 1–7 (best); Judicial independence, 1–7 (best);	NRI – WEF

Group	Variable	Measures	Source
		Efficiency of legal system in settling disputes, 1–7 (best); Efficiency of legal system in challenging regulations, 1–7 (best); Intellectual property protection, 1–7 (best); Software piracy rate, percentage software installed; Number of procedures to enforce a contract; Number of days to enforce a contract	
	Political rights and civil liberties	Political rights and civil liberties (mean of political rights and civil liberties)	Freedom House
Socioeconomic/ demographic	National income	GDP per capita (current US$)	World Development Indicator (WDI)
	Percentage of young in the population	Population ages 15–54 (% of total)	US-CIS
	Urban population	Urban population (% of total)	WDI

Index

9 780367 758615